Highland

WJ Milne
(Edited by Ian Stubbs)

ISBN 978 1905 304 189

Contents

The photographs are from the collection of Willie Milne and where known are credited as follows

ABC	Alan B Cross		
MC	Murdoch Currie	PP	Pamlin Prints
AJD	A J Douglas	PTP	Policy Transport Photos
AI	Arthur Ingram	PJR	P J Relf
RFM	R F Mack	IMGS	Ian Stubbs
IMc	Ian Maclean	GW	George F T Waugh Collection
OS	Omnibus Society		

Introduction

The history and development of The Highland Transport Company and then Highland Omnibuses is a fascinating story. The wide area of operation with a sparse population has made the Company very different from the other major Scottish operators and earned it a reputation for good financial housekeeping and conservative vehicle purchases. Needlefield workshops did a great deal of rebuilding and refurbishing of pre-war vehicles to give the fleet a more modern appearance and the first class workmanship was a credit to Highland and its staff.

From my early childhood days, being brought up and educated in the village of Ardersier, I was always fascinated by Highland's buses. They seemed to stand out as superior to those of the other operators. During the school summer holiday one year I was fascinated to see a Guy Arab II being fitted with platform doors.

Having worked as a conductor for Highland I learned a lot about the Company and as the years have passed, there are now only a few of us left who know the full story. It has been my desire to commit these memories to paper before they are lost for ever.

Acknowledgements

I would like to thank the following for articles and material to make this book possible along with my own memories and records: The Omnibus Society and the PSV Circle, whose Fleet History publications PL4 and PL5 have been invaluable as the basis for the Fleetlist, and the OS Library and Archive for some of the Timetables.

Inspector Finlay Swanson of Thurso, Jim Campbell, Peter Myres, Charles Gair, Gordon Steel, Alisdair Goodall, Traffic Officer Willie Grant and John Wares.

Photographs have been supplied by J Campbell, Alan Cross, Murdoch Currie, AJ Douglas, Arthur Ingram, Tom MacFarlane, RF Mack collection, Ian Maclean, the Omnibus Society, Policy Transport Photos, Peter J Relf, Gordon Stirling and the George FT Waugh collection in addition to those from my own collection. Inevitably, there are some from photographers whose names were not recorded. Lastly, my apologies to anyone who has supplied me with information but whose name has not been mentioned

William J Milne

Editor's note

I have been delighted to collaborate with Willie Milne in bringing the Highland story to publication. At a Venture Publications meeting we were discussing future titles and the offer of material on Highland was mentioned. It was agreed that we would like to see what was on offer and eventually a large quantity of hand-written material and photographs arrived at Glossop. I volunteered to assess the material and very quickly decided to recommend that I edit it for publication.

My love of the Scottish Highlands is well known to my friends and I have spent a part of my holidays each year since 1968 in that area. A visit to Farraline Park Bus station in Inverness was part of the holiday, in the early years I would say to my parents "I'll only be gone five minutes", often that turned into half an hour as they patiently awaited my return. The place names and locations for the photographs are all familiar to me, as are the vehicles in the fleet during those years.

Editing the material for publication has been a very pleasant trip down memory lane and an insight into the earlier years of the Company. As ever, Venture Publications are grateful for the diligent proof reading by David and Mary Shaw.

Ian Stubbs
Buxton March 2007.

This Halley Mail Car SK 183 of RS Waters ran between Wick and John O'Groats from 1913. Daniel Mowatt is the driver.

The business of Walter Wares of Castletown was taken over by Highland in 1933. SK 1178, an early vehicle, is pictured at Ingliston, Edinburgh before it became a showground. It is of a Ford 14 seater with demountable body which could be replaced by a lorry body. The owner, Walter Wares, is on the left with James Simpson on the right.

Highland History
Early Years

Inverness and District Motor Services Limited was registered on 13th April 1925 to take over the Inverness to Dingwall service operated by Henderson, formerly of Bo'ness. The service was eventually to reach Strathpeffer and Dornoch. A service to Elgin from Inverness was introduced in 1927 but was withdrawn when Northern, the established operator, threatened to invade Highland's territory elsewhere. Mr Wilmot H Fowke was the Manager and Engineer. He was one of the original Directors, a position he held until his retirement in March 1952, shortly after the formation of Highland Omnibuses Limited in February of that year.

The Railways (Road Transport) Act of 1928 enabled the London Midland & Scottish Railway to take a fifty per cent holding in Inverness and District Motor Services on 1st of December 1929. Its fleet of eighteen vehicles formed the basis of The Highland Transport Company Limited, registered on 8th April 1930 to take over Inverness and District Motor Services Limited. The new company set out to develop new services north of Inverness and to acquire established operators in the counties of Ross and Cromarty, Caithness and Sutherland which would enable a continuous service from Inverness to Wick and Thurso.

In the summer of 1930 Highland Transport acquired the Portree Coach Company Limited on the Isle of Skye, a business started in 1927 by Nicolson and running a service between Portree and Kyleakin. A service between Kyleakin and Dunvegan operated by R MacLean was also taken over at that time. Highland built up a fleet of about thirty buses, cars and lorries on Skye, the buses mainly small Albions as Inverness County Council prohibited the use of buses with more than 14 seats on Skye, a rule not relaxed until 1946 when vehicles up to 4 tons unladen weight were permitted.

The First World War had set back the development of the British motor bus and in the 1920's many continental and American buses were imported which were lightweight and fast, ideal for the competitive developing of bus routes. Messr's Knox and Hunter first linked Thurso and Wick in 1928 using an American built Reo Speedwagon. Knox and Hunter had come from Fife and had brought some of their platform staff with them to work in the north. They chose the appropriate fleetname of Pioneer and by 1930 were operating six vehicles, the official livery was blue but secondhand purchases entered service in their original colours. The partnership was ended and Knox retained the Pioneer fleetname. They became intense rivals on the Thurso to Wick service via Halkirk and Watten, undercutting each other's fares. Just three months after the formation of Highland Transport, it commenced running in opposition to Pioneer between Thurso and Wick. Highland Transport made an application to build a garage in Janet Street, Thurso on land owned by the LMS railway but this met with objections from some of the residents including two former Provosts of Thurso who feared that the building of a garage would lead to increased noise and pollution. At a special meeting of Thurso Town Council in August 1930 Mr Wilmot H Fowke, Highland's General Manager, stated that services were bound to develop around Thurso, providing no obstacles were put in the way and this would increase the prosperity of the town. The objections were overruled and unanimous consent was given to the construction of a garage. Originally built to accommodate three buses this garage still exists today as the body repair shop of Highland Country Bus division of the Rapson group who bought Highland Omnibuses on privatisation in 1991.

Shortly after commencing operations in Caithness, Highland Transport introduced two new services which are still operated by Highland Country. The first was a Sunday afternoon excursion to John O'Groats for the price of 3/6d (17.5p) and a Saturday only journey from Wick to Thurso via Castletown, departing at 10.30 as it still does today. With more buses converging

Bobby Duff and James Davison with the Pioneer Reo Speedwagon in Town Hall Square, Thurso.

on the restricted town centres of Wick and Thurso, congestion was inevitable and at Wick it was recommended that buses divert off the narrow High Street to wait at the Riverside parking stance, although they were permitted to wait for a maximum of ten minutes to collect passengers in the town centre. In Thurso there were a number of terminal points used by the different operators. Highland Transport used the Town Hall, David Henderson and Walter Wares used Anderson's the ironmongers, Alex Robertson and James Begg used D Sutherland the bakers, George S Begg and Donald Allan used Shearers the grocers, William Johnstone used Budge the draper and Black of Watten used Lindsay the ironmonger. The siting of these terminals caused much congestion, particularly around St John's Square, and in 1932 Thurso Town Council ruled that all buses should use the Town Hall as a central bus terminus. Promoting their services with the slogan 'Civility and Reliability', Highland Transport was intent on providing an efficient and reliable service which they hoped would lead to increased local trade. On weekdays fifteen return journeys were advertised, six via Castletown and the remainder via Halkirk and Watten. The journey time was a generous eighty minutes compared with the present fifty five minutes, but one must take into account the low performance of the vehicles which were restricted to a maximum speed of 30 mph. A limited Sunday timetable consisted of three return journeys.

Highland Transport consolidated its position in Caithness by acquiring smaller operators. T Hunter of Castletown, Knox's former partner in Pioneer, sold out to Highland in 1931 and his bus, SK 1507, an Albion PK with Spicer B26F body, became Highland Transport No. 53. In August 1932, JJ Robertson of Wick (A Robertson & Son) was acquired along with six vehicles, four Chevrolets, one AJS Pilot and an Albion PKA26, all of which entered Highland service. Further acquisitions were W Johnstone of Castletown in May 1933, W Wares of Castletown in the same year,

Number SK 1467, a 1928 Bean parked outside Barristons Garage, Thurso with Walter Wares on the left. This vehicle had been withdrawn before the sale to Highland.

Walter Wares' 1930 Reo Speedwagon SK 1640 with 20 seat body had been disposed of before the business was sold to Highland, but another two Reo's did join the Highland fleet in 1933.

Inverness & District operated this 18 seat Cowieson-bodied Albion PF26 which was new in 1926. Number 29 passed to Highland Transport Co. Ltd. In 1930 and was withdrawn in 1934.

J Begg (Express Motor Company), Port Dunbar, Wick in May 1933 and D Allan & Son, Watten in December that year.

The slow, inconvenient and infrequent train service between Wick and Thurso persuaded many people to forsake the train for the bus; however, the LMS did try to encourage weekend travel by offering a direct Saturday excursion for a return fare of one shilling (5p). The LMS holding in Highland Transport meant that bus and rail tickets were interchangeable but in November 1932 they objected in vain to Highland and W Wares reducing the cost of their season tickets between Wick and Thurso, claiming they were undercutting the railway fares. However much the buses must have reduced the railway company's revenue in Caithness, the recognised means of travel to the south was still the train. It was possible to travel to Inverness by bus but this meant catching the 8.10am Wick to Helmsdale mail car and then changing for Dornoch where another change was necessary to reach Inverness at 4.17pm.

In 1935 Highland Transport decided to concentrate their efforts on the mainland and sold their Skye services to other local operators. Nicolson's, trading as The Skye Transport Company, took over some routes, they in turn sold out to the Scottish Co-operative Wholesale Society in 1946 and then traded as Skye Transport until bought by David MacBrayne on 28th November 1958. Highland returned to the Isle of Skye after 31 years when in 1966 it acquired the tours and excursions licences of John Lochart of Portree. From May to September 1969 a Saturday only service from Portree to Edinburgh was jointly operated by Highland Omnibuses and Scottish Omnibuses with a journey time of nine hours. The restrictions on size of vehicles had long since been lifted and 36 foot long AEC Reliances, Leylands and Bristols made their appearance on the Island.

In 1938 a conductor's remuneration was £1 per week and a driver could earn £3 after two years service. On weekdays they were expected to work 12 hours and there was no overtime pay. Following the declaration of war on 3rd September 1939 the Royal Navy fleet was stationed at Scapa Flow in the Orkneys and thousands of personnel were sent north by train to Thurso and transported by bus to the ferry at Scrabster pier, two miles from Thurso.

Knox & Hunter's 'Pioneer' service was running between Wick and Thurso from 1928. After the sale to Highland in 1931 No. 53, a Spicer-bodied Albion PK26, is behind driver Jimmy Davidson and is parked at Thurso garage next to former Inverness & District No. 40, an Albion PJ26, with driver Bobby Cormack.

Inverness & District purchased this Albion PJ26 which is seen operating in Caithness as Highland No. 41.

The Royal Hotel in Thurso also operated this journey taking guests to the pier. It was allocated a Bedford OWB to assist in the troop movements. Two large airfields were constructed at Castletown and Wick for the Royal Air Force and these brought extra business to Highland Transport during the war years. The allocation of five Albions at Thurso was augmented in 1942 by a solitary Tilling Stevens with Willowbrook B26F body, originally built for export, which took fleetnumber 1 and lasted until 1955, becoming T1 in the Highland Omnibuses fleet. No. 2 was a Leyland Tiger TS11 with a Willowbrook B36F body and was the most mechanically advanced bus in Caithness at the time. It became H2 in the Highland Omnibuses fleet and saw service until 1957. For a period Wick was the home to a Gilford HSG which had been modified to run on producer gas. The bus had been built in 1937 by High Speed Gas (GB) Ltd. The chassis was extensively tested in Scotland and performed impressively enough to persuade Highland to buy it. The chassis was modified to run on peat and a Cowieson body fitted, becoming No. 76.

In 1946 James Wilson's Thurso to Mey mail car service was acquired along with a Duple-bodied Bedford OWB, SK 2862, which became Highland No. 8 and served Highland Omnibuses as their C8 until 1960. It was sold to J S Moncrieff of Spiggie and then in December 1962 to Shetland operator A J Eunion of Virkie where it survived until April 1966. Wilson's mail service to the west had passed to O'Brien of Bettyhill in 1939 and had latterly used two 2-ton Ford vehicles. The long established Wick to John O'Groats service of Robert Simon Waters of Wick was also taken over in 1946.

The need for vehicles with a larger capacity on the Thurso to Wick service lead to the arrival of the first double-deckers in Caithness in 1946. These were Guy Arab Mark IIs with lowbridge utility bodies by Northern Counties seating 55, being numbered 19 and 20, registration marks AST 957/8. Latterly, as E19/20, these served in Caithness until 1963/4. E20 had the unusual distinction of a Highland double-decker

giving further service in Edinburgh from May until July 1963, covering a shortage of vehicles in the Scottish Omnibuses fleet.

Expansion continued in the Inverness area in 1937 with the takeover of Fraser Brothers of Kirkhill and their services to Muir of Ord, Beauly and Inverness. Seven vehicles were acquired, three Reos becoming Highland's Nos. 78, 87 and 88 (ST 6361/5535/6604), a 14 seat Chevrolet, No. 77 (ST 6461), two AEC Regal IV with B32R bodies by Park Royal and Walker, Nos.84/85 (ST 7318/7851) and a 30 seat Albion PK115 taking No. 86 (ST 8167).

The British Transport Commission (BTC) was established under the 1947 Transport Act, taking over the fifty per cent railway holding in Highland Transport from 1st January 1948. Mr W H Fowke was due to retire in 1951 and it was agreed to sell the remaining shareholding to the BTC. Management passed to Scottish Omnibuses Limited of Edinburgh, another BTC company set up on 4th April 1949 to take over the operations of Scottish Motor Traction Limited (SMT) of Edinburgh. Mr Fowke delayed his retirement until March 1952 providing day to day management at Inverness until Highland Omnibuses Limited took over.

The earliest record of public road transport in Inverness dates from 1836 when George Crotchie introduced a two horse omnibus from the Exchange to South Kessock where it connected with the ferry across to North Kessock on the Black Isle. From the summer of 1836 until c1839 there was a horse bus from Cromarty to Inverness via Rosemarkie, Avoch and the Kessock ferry. Also on record is the "Caberfeidh" coach from Dingwall to Inverness and it is believed that this service also used the ferry. All these services were short lived but the Inverness to South Kessock route was revived in 1881 by John Grant and Company who also ran from the town centre to Island Bank Road on the south side of the town. Both these services were acquired by Macrae & Dick in 1882, immediately withdrawing the Island Bank road route and only running to the Kessock ferry on market

PARCEL RATES.

PARCELS CARRIED AT OWNERS' RISK.

	s. d.		s. d.
1 to 3 lbs.	0 4	25 to 34 lbs. ...	1 0
4 to 7 lbs.	0 6	35 to 44 lbs. ...	1 2
8 to 14 lbs.	0 8	45 to 54 lbs. ...	1 4
15 to 24 lbs.	0 10	55 to 60 lbs. ...	1 6

Fractions of a lb. are charged as 1 lb.

All Parcels must be Prepaid.

The Company will not accept responsibility for delays arising through break-down, or from any other unavoidable cause.

This Notice is issued subject to the Company's Bye-Laws.

INVERNESS, *August, 1925.*

INVERNESS & DISTRICT

MOTOR SERVICES

LIMITED

TO ALL PARTS BY ARRANGEMENT.

TIME TABLE

FOR

DINGWALL & TAIN SERVICE

WITH

LIST of FARES and other particulars.

PARTIES of 12 and upwards may be Booked by Special Arrangement for any distance.

For TERMS and ENQUIRIES apply :—

ENQUIRY OFFICE,

BANK STREET, INVERNESS.

Tel. No. 371.

CHRONICLE, INVERNESS.

William Davidson

PASSENGER FARES.

INVERNESS to—	s. d.	DINGWALL to	s. d.
Clachnaharry .	0 3	Maryburgh . .	0 3
Bunchrew . .	0 5	Conon	0 6
Lentran . . .	0 8	Balavil . . .	0 6
Bogroy . . .	0 10	Highfield . . .	0 8
Moniack . . .	0 10	Muir of Ord . .	0 10
Ballindoune . .	1 0	Beauly . . .	1 3
Beauly	1 3	Ballindoune . .	1 6
Muir of Ord . .	1 8	Moniack . . .	1 8
Highfield . . .	2 0	Bogroy . . .	1 8
Balavil . . .	2 0	Lentran . . .	2 0
Conon	2 0	Bunchrew . . .	2 0
Maryburgh . .	2 4	Clachnaharry .	2 4
DINGWALL . .	2 4	INVERNESS .	2 4

Persons boarding 'Bus between regular stopping places are charged from previous stop.

PARCEL RATE.

PARCELS CARRIED AT OWNERS' RISK.

	s. d.		s. d.
1 to 3 lbs.	0 4	25 to 34 lbs. ...	1 0
4 to 7 lbs.	0 6	35 to 44 lbs. ...	1 2
8 to 14 lbs.	0 8	45 to 54 lbs. ...	1 4
15 to 24 lbs.	0 10	55 to 60 lbs. ...	1 6

Fractions of a lb. are charged as 1 lb.

NOTE.—We will not be held responsible for delays through breakdown of Cars or any other unavoidable cause.

INVERNESS & DISTRICT

MOTOR SERVICES

LIMITED

TO ALL PARTS BY ARRANGEMENT.

TIME TABLE

FOR

INVERNESS and DINGWALL SERVICE

WITH

LIST of FARES and other particulars.

PARTIES of 12 and upwards may be Booked by Special Arrangement for any distance.

For TERMS and ENQUIRIES apply :—

ENQUIRY OFFICE,

BANK STREET, INVERNESS.

Tel. No. 371.

CHRONICLE, INVERNESS.

Bank Street in Inverness is the location of this AEC Regal with 32 seat Porteous body about to depart for Strathpeffer. (OS)

Highland acquired this ex-demonstrator AEC Regent with Strachan highbridge body in 1933 which is also seen in Bank Street, Inverness. (PP)

Albion Valkyrie with Cowieson body heading for John O'Groats in 1952. Number A59 had been rebuilt and reseated to B34R by Highland Transport and fitted with a Gardner 5LW engine. The Eagle motif which can be seen was to become a feature of the livery. (ABC)

Sister vehicle No. A61 had also been rebuilt but to B34F layout. The Eagle motif which was used for many years can be clearly seen in this 1952 photograph. (ABC)

days, Tuesday and Friday. In 1873 Macrae & Dick were providing facilities for the tourist with horse drawn carriages operating to many local beauty spots. The first motor bus was purchased in 1910 and the touring business expanded rapidly only to be brought to a halt by the war in 1914. After the war the touring business resumed and a number of bus services introduced to Nairn, Culloden, Tomatin and Fort William.

The company operated a fleet of twenty vehicles, mainly Austins, Albions and Bedfords. The fleet livery was cream and chocolate. In 1951 the BTC took over the omnibus operations of Macrae & Dick Limited, leaving the motor dealership to continue under that name. Highland Transport applied to take over vehicles and licences on behalf of the BTC this being granted in December 1951.

In January 1952 Highland Transport applied for the Inverness to Nairn and Inverness to Kerrowaird services of W Alexander & Sons Limited, together with excursions and tours from Inverness. Included in this application were the ex-Greig Inverness town service and the former Wemyss Brothers of Ardersier service from Fort George to Inverness. The application was withdrawn shortly afterwards. The Wemyss brothers had started their business in the early 1930's with services from Fort George barracks and Dalcross RAF camp to Inverness. A lot of their work came from Private Hires and on the Saturday in August of the Nairn Games they operated a special service from Ardersier to and from Nairn. The business was sold to W Alexander & Sons Limited on 26th June 1950.

Munro and MacLennan introduced a chain driven 32 hp Albion to the South Kessock route circa 1914 but by 1919 MacLennan was operating in his name only. Shortly afterward he met competition from the Mackenzie brothers who used a Mercedes-Daimler on their service. The Mackenzies soon faded out of the picture but the proprietors of the Kessock ferry, the MacDonald brothers, took up the challenge and introduced a Riker bus and later a Hawkeye. MacLennan survived the competition, modernised his

fleet and in 1927 sold out to his conductor, William Greig. In 1930 Greig purchased the MacDonald brothers share in the Kessock service and thereby removed all competition. The service had relied on the ferry passengers for its survival but at about this time the Royal Burgh of Inverness built a housing estate within half a mile of the ferry terminal and this in due course provided welcome additional revenue. Further expansion took place within the Burgh and William Greig virtually became the sole provider of the Inverness town services. On 17th November 1947 Greig sold his business to W Alexander & Sons Limited, effective from 6th December that year, but retained a coachbuilding business in Telford Street, Inverness. W Alexander & Sons Limited was no new operator to the area as they came in to the Highland capital from Elgin, Macduff and Aberdeen; in summer there was a route from Glasgow. Alexanders also aquired Greig's garage on Carse Road and some twenty vehicles which were quickly replaced by their own vehicles, although the Greig's Guy Arabs were transferred to the Fife area where they continued in service until the mid 1960's.

Albion Valkyries Nos. 60, 61 and 62 when new in Dornoch depot. The slight difference in the shape of the windscreen of No. 62 can be seen.

Highland's first 6 wheeler was No. A79, an Albion PR145 with Cowieson B40R body. (OS)

Number 76 displaying the attachments for its 'High Speed Gas' power.

A rear view of the Gas powered Gilford No. 76. Note the ventilation louvres.

Frasers 'Pullman' Services were taken over in 1938 by Highland. This 1933 view shows ST 7318 a recently delivered Park Royal-bodied AEC Regal IV.

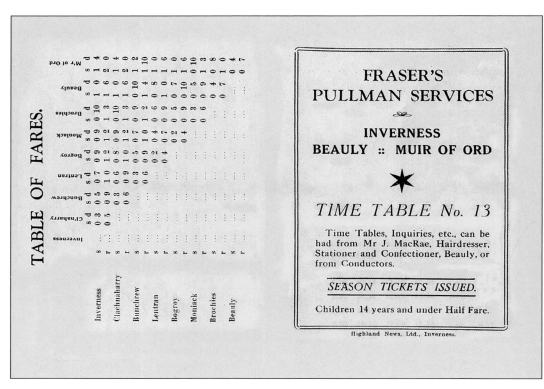

TABLE OF FARES.

FRASER'S PULLMAN SERVICES

INVERNESS
BEAULY :: MUIR OF ORD

★

TIME TABLE No. 13

Time Tables, Inquiries, etc., can be had from Mr J. MacRae, Hairdresser, Stationer and Confectioner, Beauly, or from Conductors.

SEASON TICKETS ISSUED.

Children 14 years and under Half Fare.

Highland News, Ltd., Inverness.

An unusual purchase was this TSM with Willowbrook B26F body. Number T1 is shown turning into Traill Street in Thurso. After withdrawal in 1956 it became a goods vehicle. (ABC)

Number H2, Willowbrook-bodied Leyland TS11 is in Nairn bus station ready to work the Inverness route through the villages of Croy, Cawdor and Culloden.

This 1942 SMT-bodied Bedford OWB, was extensively rebuilt by Scottish Omnibuses and is pictured outside Highland's Thurso office. (OS)

Highland Omnibuses Limited

The reason for withdrawing the application for the Alexander Inverness based services was the formation of the new company, Highland Omnibuses Limited, combining The Highland Transport Company Limited and the Macrae & Dick business as one operating unit with effect from 11th February 1952. In March 1952 Highland Omnibuses Limited submitted their application for the Alexander services together with a new application for the Highland Transport services, both of which were granted in May 1952. The John O'Groats to Wick Royal Mail service was acquired in September 1952 from William Mawatt who was the driver of the service and also operated it on behalf of Robert Simon Waters of Wick. This was a route which had first operated as far back as 1912. One of the first Mail buses was a chain driven, solid tyre 25 hp Halley (SK 183) which had been bodied by Malcolm Brothers of Whitechapel, Wick.

The side panels of the bus bore the 'GR' crest of King George V. The Halley was painted blue and driven by Daniel Mawatt until his retirement, always being known as 'Denniel's Bus'. His son, William, continued the service, at first with a Ford 16 seater new in 1934 (SK 1952) and later with a new Bedford OB/Duple B28F (SK 2840) which continued in service as Highland C24 until 1959.

When Scottish Omnibuses took over the old Highland Transport Company they could hardly have been accused of doing so with a view of immediate profits. The objective was to extend the consistent service that was already being provided in Scotland. Mr James Amos, the group Chairman, pointed out at a Traffic Commissioners' hearing that, if it were not for the benefits of the link with other fleets in the group, Highland would not be able to provide services required by the public.

1944 Bedford OWB with SMT B32F body at Farraline Park bus station in Inverness. Number 15 is about to depart on a local service to Holm Mills, the weaving factory of James Pringle Ltd. This bus was to be rebodied as a coach in 1953. (ABC)

Three SMT-bodied Bedford OWB's were delivered in 1942. Number C5 is shown with a new Burlingham Baby Seagull body having been converted to normal control. (IMc)

The revenue per mile in 1956 was 18.97d, below the operating costs of 20.71d for the Stage Carriage services and fare increases were necessary. Tours and Contract work supplemented the Stage Carriage revenue. Mr Amos continued, "I have been asked many times why we wish to extend our interests at all to Inverness and the Highlands. I can tell you in a few simple words, it is because we believe the group's interest in road passenger transport not only serve the commercial interests of industrial areas but, not less importantly, the well being and prosperity of Scotland and the Scottish people. To provide adequate services in so sparsely populated an area, with the constant accompaniment of rising costs has been the perennial problem facing officials. Perhaps many of the people of the Highlands have no clear idea of what they may reasonably expect for their money, but there is no doubt that in present circumstances they are receiving at least average value as the transport world accounts for it.

Throughout, the policy has been to take into reckoning local conditions and local feelings, so service alterations have been undertaken only after most careful consideration. Although the system has been streamlined in accordance with modern needs, the Highland bus is still essentially a local bus. In spite of progressive integration of resources within the group, there has been no mass migration of officials from the Scottish capital to the north. To the outsider it is obvious that the system is still running with the same friendliness that characterised it in earlier years.

The Highland Omnibuses system is not operated from Edinburgh, but from its traditional headquarters in Inverness, decisions are taken by men on the spot and similar arrangements apply at lower levels of management. Mr N R Sutherland, manager of Highland Omnibuses Ltd is responsible for services in area covering some 100,000 square miles, taking in John O'Groats in the north, Nairn in the east, Fort William in the south and Strathpeffer on the western side. Stage services are

now running an average of 50,000 miles weekly. The touring section of the fleet, which is an important revenue earner, covers about 250,000 miles a year. Two District Traffic Superintendents share the ordinary supervision, one of them taking in the area north of Helmsdale and the other the services from that point to the south. All over the area good work has been done in ironing out difficulties and co-ordinating the fare scale with that of the rest of the group. Originally, fares had been set on a somewhat free and easy basis, so that the rationalisation process left a minority of passengers a trifle upset because they no longer enjoyed individual advantages derived from the inconsistencies.

With the introduction of a fares structure of the acceptable type, in which distances between the stages are more or less equal, new ticketing machines have been introduced. Those on the Inverness town services are of Ultimate manufacture, whilst on the country routes Setright machines are now employed."

A considerable expansion of services in Caithness took place in late 1954 when the United Kingdom Atomic Energy Authority started the construction of the Dounreay Experimental Reactor Establishment (DERE) about ten miles west of Thurso. Additional buses were required to provide workman's services to the construction site and six Leyland TS8s were obtained from Central SMT for this purpose. In 1955 three Guy Arabs arrived from Scottish Omnibuses to expand these services, although they were not confined to the Dounreay services as older buses in the fleet were cascaded to serve Dounreay. As the pace of construction quickened further buses were required and sent to Caithness including ten Utility Guy Arabs obtained from David Lawson in 1956, four more from Western SMT. and another four from David Lawson in 1957. At the peak of construction more than forty buses were required to maintain the services. Many of the utility Guys were withdrawn from service as construction neared completion in 1958.

This Bedford OWB with Duple body was originally allocated to Wilson (The Royal Hotel) Thurso for use in the transporting of Naval personnel from Thurso to Scrabster harbour. It became No. C8 in the Highland fleet in 1946. It is followed by No. 20 a Northern Counties-bodied Guy Arab II. (IMc)

At Dingwall bus station, Guy Arab No. E20 displays its platform doors. (ABC)

THE HIGHLAND TRANSPORT COMPANY LIMITED.

Enquiry Office and Parcels Depots:—

Thurso—35 High St. Phone 90   Wick—6 Back Bridge St. Phone 127

Head Office: Old National Bldgs, Inverness.   Phone Inverness 371

CAITHNESS SERVICES

Emergency

TIME TABLE No. 215

From Monday 29th January, 1940

(Subject to alteration)

**For Main Road and Black Isle Services
See separate Time Table**

While every endeavour is made to adhere to these times, the Company will not accept responsibility for delays arising through breakdown or other unavoidable cause.

Issued subject to the Company's General Conditions, and to the Regulations and Conditions laid down by the Roads Traffic Acts.

Parcels are conveyed at Owner's Risk and must be pre-paid. They must be handed in to the local Parcel Agent or where there is no Agent, to a Conductor and a receipt obtained in either case.

W. H. FOWKE, *Manager.*

HUNA and MEY to THURSO / CASTLETOWN and MEY to WICK.

		Tues a.m.	Sat. p.m.	Thur p.m.			Thur a.m.	Tues p.m.	Sat. p.m.
Wick	dep	...	...	4 0	Thurso	dep	9 0	4 0	8 0
Keiss		...	...	4 25	Castletown	,,	9 10	4 20	8 20
Huna	dep	9 30	...	...	Dunnet	,,	9 10	4 35	8 35
Canisbay		9 35	...	4 50	Brough	,,			
Mey		10 0	1 0	5 10	Barrock Road	,,	9 20	4 50	8 50
Scarfskerry		10 10	1 10	5 20	Barrock Ch.	,,			
Barrock Road		...	...	5 30	Scarfskerry	,,	9 30	5 0	9 0
Barrock Ch.					Mey	,,	9 40	5 10	9 0
Brough		10 23	1 23	...	Canisbay	,,	10 0	5 30	9 10
Dunnet		10 35	1 35	5 40	Huna	,,	10 25	5 35	...
Castletown		10 40	1 40	5 50	Keiss	,,	10 25		
Thurso	arr	11 10	2 10	6 10	Wick	arr	10 50		

WICK—STAXIGOE. Saturdays only.

		p.m.	p.m.			p.m.	p.m.
Wick	dep	1 30	5 10	Staxigoe	dep	1 45	5 25
Staxigoe	arr	1 44	5 24	Wick	arr	2 0	5 40

WICK LOCAL SERVICE.

Bridge Street, Dempster Street, Argyle Square, Macrae Street, Cairndhuna Terrace, Huddart Street, Breadalbane Terrace, Sinclair Terrace, and West Banks.

Bridge Street; dep—	via		Bridge Street; arr—	via
12 29 p.m.	WB (SE)		12 45 p.m.	B (SE)
N 1 5 p.m.	B		1 19 p.m.	A
3 0 p.m.	A		3 14 p.m.	A
5 15 p.m.	B		5 29 p.m.	A
7 30 p.m.	A (SO)		7 44 p.m.	B (SO)

A—via Argyle Square.   B—via Breadalbane Terrace.   WB—via West Banks.
SE—Saturdays excepted   SO—Sats. only.   N—Not after 1.5 p.m. on Weds.

The Sutherland Transport & Trading Company Limited abandoned its loss making, non mail carrying services from Lairg to Bonar Bridge and Lairg to Golspie, which were taken over by Highland Omnibuses in April 1956. Both routes ran parallel with the railway and competed with it. On 13th June 1960 British Railways Scottish Region closed twenty or more stations between Inverness and Wick including the branch line to Dornoch. Highland Omnibuses responded by providing improved or replacement services throughout the area.

In June 1957 a new bus station was opened in the centre of Inverness at Farraline Park which handled 300 daily departures including those of David MacBrayne and Alexanders. The station covered 19,500 square feet with nine departure bays. There were also booking and enquiry offices, administrative offices and all the usual public facilities.

At the official opening, coaches from the Highland Omnibuses fleet were prominent in the display of vehicles. These coaches earned important additional revenue for the Company operating tours to Balmoral, Fort William and the remoter parts of North West Scotland, Loch Maree, Ullapool, Lochinver, Durness and Tongue.

One service that was popular with tourists was Inverness to Scrabster to connect with ferry to the Orkneys. When this service started in 1952 passengers numbered 3,905, this increased by fifty per cent the following year and was followed by a steady increase in subsequent years. Many of the day tours involved early starts, returning to Inverness in the late evening. Distances covered were quite large but journeys were slow because most of the highland roads were single track with passing places. The massive road building schemes begun in the late 1960's, and still continuing, have made many journeys unrecognisable today.

In 1961 the BTC formed a new Holding Company, Scottish Omnibuses Group Holdings Limited, operative from 9th May. The shareholdings of the following companies were transferred to the new company: W Alexander & Sons Limited;

Scottish Omnibuses Limited; Central SMT. Company Limited; Western SMT Company Limited; Highland Omnibuses Limited; David Lawson Limited and The SMT Insurance Company Limited. The Transport Act of 1962 abolished the BTC and formed the Transport Holding Company (THC) to oversee road and bus interests. Scottish Omnibuses Group Holdings Limited was taken over by the THC and in 1963 its name changed to Scottish Bus Group Limited.

The Garve Hotel had been owned by the Mackenzie family for 115 years and was put up for sale in 1964, the unlikely buyer being the Scottish Bus Group who continued ownership until 1977. Associated with the hotel were the bus operations licensed to WD Mackenzie which were transferred to Highland Omnibuses giving them a mail bus service between Garve station and Ullapool, and an occasional service from Ullapool to Inverness. Nineteen Sixty-Four saw the acquisition of a few more small operators. D McKay and Sons of Tain was taken over early in 1964, they operated services from Tain to Portmahomack, Nigg Ferry and Alness. None of the vehicles taken over operated for Highland Omnibuses. The next acquisition included one vehicle and routes from Gairloch, Aultbea and Laide to Inverness from J & NMB Bain (J Bain & Son) of North Erradale, Gairloch. The bus was an Albion FT3AB/Duple C31F. This business had been established in the early 1930s with routes from Gairloch to Ullapool and Aultbea to Inverness as well as a local service from Gairloch to Melvaig. During the 1950s there were Private Hires transporting fishermen working off the West Coast to and from their homes in the fishing ports on the Moray Firth. After the sale to Highland, Bain retained one local service and some school contracts but finally gave up the bus side of the business in the early 1980s. In May 1964 the business of WJ Ross, Balblair was taken over with the routes to Dingwall from Resolis (Wednesday and Saturday) and Resolis to Inverness (Tuesday and Friday). Two vehicles were acquired, another Albion FT3AB but with Strachan C31F body and a Bedford SB/Duple C33F. In October James

Guy Arab E20 was to serve in Edinburgh after being withdrawn by Highland. It is seen in St Andrews bus station with the paper stickers showing 'on hire to SOL Ltd'. (AJD)

Displaying the wooden slatted seats of its Weymann lowbridge body, utility Guy Arab No. E24 is at Dingwall Station. (OS)

Number E35 was the first of the four Strachan-bodied Guy Arabs and this view in Wick shows the platform doors which had been fitted in 1950. (ABC)

Number E38 is shown on the Thurso to Wick via Castletown service.

AULTBEA — INVERNESS
BUS SERVICE
(SEASON 1955)

ALTERNATE THURSDAYS, 12th MAY to 27th OCTOBER

also

EXCURSION ON ALTERNATE SATURDAYS, 2nd JULY to 24th SEPTEMBER

MAY	JUNE	JULY
		SAT. 2nd
THURS. 12th	THURS. 9th	THURS. 7th
		SAT. 16th
THURS. 26th	THURS. 23rd	THURS. 21st
		SAT. 30th

AUGUST	SEPTEMBER	OCTOBER
THURS. 4th	THURS. 1st	
SAT. 13th	SAT. 10th	THURS. 13th
THURS. 18th	THURS. 15th	
SAT. 27th	SAT. 24th	THURS. 27th
	THURS. 29th	

TIME TABLE

OUTWARD—

MELLON CHARLES	depart	7 0 a.m.
AULTBEA	„	7 10 a.m.
POOLEWE	„	7 30 a.m.
GAIRLOCH (Strath)	„	7 50 a.m.
LOCH MAREE	„	8 20 a.m.
KINLOCHEWE	„	8 45 a.m.
INVERNESS (Church St.)	arrive	11 20 a.m.

INWARD—

INVERNESS (Church St.)	depart	6 0 p.m.
KINLOCHEWE	arrive	8 40 p.m.
LOCH MAREE	„	9 0 p.m.
GAIRLOCH (Strath)	„	9 30 p.m.
POOLEWE	„	9 50 p.m.
AULTBEA	„	10 10 p.m.
MELLON CHARLES	„	10 20 p.m.

FARES

	Single	Return
MELLON CHARLES, AULTBEA and POOLEWE to INVERNESS	12/-	20/-
GAIRLOCH to INVERNESS	10/-	17/6
LOCH MAREE and KINLOCHEWE to INVERNESS	8/-	15/-

JOHN BAIN & SONS
NORTH ERRADALE
Phone: GAIRLOCH 45

McKintosh, Cantraywood, Croy was taken over with a Bedford OB/SMT C29F and the route from Croy to Inverness which operated on Tuesday, Friday and Saturday. At one time this service ran in competition with Macrae & Dick's route from Inverness to Nairn via Croy. In April 1934 James McKintosh started a bus service between Croy and Inverness with a 14 seater Ford, ST 7657. During the war years a Thursday only service was run from Croy to Nairn via Clunas and from Inverness to Balloch. Further acquisitions came in 1965 with the March purchase of the bus side of the Achnasheen Hotel Company Limited, a mail bus service from Achnasheen to Laide and Diabeg and a service from Laide to Inverness which operated on alternate Thursdays with former John Bain service already operated by Highland Omnibuses. Five vehicles were acquired including a Land Rover. Seven vehicles were bought in October 1965 with the business of Fred Newton, West End Garage, Dingwall which consisted of school services and Private Hire work.

Expansion to the south of Inverness came in December 1966 with the acquisition of the bus business of Norman Smith of Grantown-on-Spey. This had been established ten years earlier to pioneer the ski-bus business in the Cairngorm Mountains. At the end of 1965 Highland Omnibuses had applied to operate three services for skiers in the Aviemore area but this had been opposed by Norman Smith. The May 1966 Traffic Court hearing was adjourned and continued in September when the application was refused in favour of Norman Smith, the established operator. A few weeks later it was announced that Highland had purchased the Smith business. To operate the ski services Highland acquired six Leyland Royal Tigers from Ribble which, after a short period of service, had their rear ends rebuilt by Walter Alexander (Coachbuilders) Limited to create a platform to carry skis. This gave them an appearance not unlike the buses of Paris operated by RATP The business of Peter Burr, Tongue was also bought in 1966 and an application was made in September to operate his mail-bus service from Tongue to Thurso

which for unknown reasons was rejected. Highland then formed a new subsidiary company, Peter Burr (Omnibuses) Limited, with a registered office of Farraline Park, Inverness and this company took over the operation of the route on 10th July 1967.

This company continued as a subsidiary of the Scottish Transport Group. Dornoch operator Seaforth McGregor was taken over in May 1967 along with three vehicles which had operated school journeys and a local Sunday service. Next to be acquired was R Robertson of Strathglass, in August with two vehicles which ran the route from Beauly to Tomich.

A new Bus Station in Nairn was opened on 6th December 1967 which included garage and office accommodation which replaced the rented garage space at Knowell & Cummings and the office space within McRae's travel agency in Nairn High Street. In June 1968 R Kennedy was acquired with a Tuesday and Friday only service from Glenconvinth to Inverness. Bob Kennedy, as he was known, had in earlier years arranged for his bus to meet with the Highland Transport Company service at Brockies Corner on the A9 to collect passengers for the Glenconvinth area.

TO TICKET-HOLDERS.

All Monthly Tickets issued from First of each Month.

Northern Counties-bodied Guy Arab II, No. 51 is seen when new in Academy Street, Inverness awaiting its departure for Dornoch. The vehicle behind is Weymann-bodied Guy Arab II, No. 25 which is heading for Dingwall.

This 1963 view of No. E51 shows the effects of a rebuild in 1961.

A rear view of Northern Counties-bodied Guy Arab II, No. 47 and Strachan-bodied No. 37 in Beauly also shows an Albion CX9 with Brockhouse body belonging to Robertson of Strathglass. (ABC)

Three Strachan-bodied Guy Arab II single-deckers arrived in 1947. Number 43 is pictured leaving Strachans coachworks in London.

At Muir Of Ord is No. 63, another of the Northern Counties-bodied Guy Arab IIs. (ABC)

At Farraline Park Guy Arab No. E64 displays the platform doors fitted by Scottish Omnibuses in January 1960 to its Northern Counties body. It was working out of Nairn depot for a few weeks before returning to Caithness. It was the only vehicle of the batch to retain its original green leather seat covering throughout its working life.

Guy Arab III, No. K86 is outside Wick depot and is carrying a second-hand Alexander coach body which was fitted in 1955 to replace the original Strachan body. (RFM)

MOTOR COACH TOURS
from
INVERNESS
HIGHLAND OMNIBUSES LIMITED
Season 1952

The Scottish Transport Group Years

The 1968 Transport Act created the Scottish Transport Group which came into being on 1st January 1969. This new group controlled the Scottish Bus Group, The Caledonian Steam Packet Company Limited and the THC half share in David MacBrayne Limited. In July 1969 full control of MacBrayne's passed to the Scottish Transport Group. Rationalisation of bus services followed with Highland Omnibuses gaining the majority of MacBrayne's services and vehicles.

An unexpected development was the transfer from W Alexander & Sons (Midland) of their Oban garage and services to Highland Omnibuses. This resulted in the Glasgow to Oban service operated by Midland and the Oban to Fort William service of MacBrayne becoming jointly operated by Highland and Midland. The Oban to Ardrishaig service ex-MacBrayne became jointly run by Highland and Western SMT.

Following this period of rapid expansion it was necessary for Highland to look at

Number 83 was also fitted with a replacement Alexander coach body in 1958 and is seen here in coach livery when new with Strachan coachwork.

Passing through Lewiston on its way to Fort Augustus is GJ 2391 a Thurgood-bodied Chevrolet LQ. It was new to HJ Phillips of London in 1930 and passed to Macrae & Dick in1932. It was withdrawn before the sale to Highland in 1952.

the unremunerative areas, a clearer picture emerging now that the former MacBrayne's bus services were accounted for separately from the shipping. In the spring of 1971 Allan MacDonald of Kinlochmoidart took over operation of two former MacBrayne's services, Ardgour to Kinlochmoidart and Kilchoan to Acharacle. Also withdrawn at that time was the overnight mail bus service from Fort William to Kingussie which had been operated by an 8 seat Bedford. Soon after, Highland applied to withdraw more services including Tain to Nigg Ferry and former MacBrayne's Kyle of Lochalsh to Glenelg, Isle of Skye routes Portree to Peinchorran and Fairybridge to Geary. Approval was given by the Traffic Commissioners to withdraw in April but negotiations continued with the County Councils in respect of retaining the services with subsidies. On 10th July Clan Garage, Kyle of Lochalsh and Davidson of Glenelg were granted short term licences to operate the Kyle of Lochalsh to Glenelg service in two sections. Highland withdrew on 17th July and from 19th July Clan started

to operate from Kyle of Lochalsh to Letterfearn and Davidson from Glenelg to Shiel Bridge.

Fortrose depot closed in February 1972 and vehicles and operations transferred to Dingwall. A new depot at Seafield Road, Inverness was opened on 20th July by the Provost, WA Smith. The new depot had space for over 100 vehicles with covered accommodation for maintenance, washing, cleaning and refuelling. The Head Office was transferred from Farraline Park to Seafield Road at the same time. The depot included a new system of forced hot air pre-heating of vehicles before taking up duty in the winter months. Drivers had to take care to uncouple the flexible ducts before setting off. On occasions when the driver forgot, there was the sight of a bus with a tail roaming the streets of Inverness!

On 26th March 1973 after many years of argument and deliberation, a new roll-on, roll-off ferry service was introduced from Ullapool to Stornaway on the Isle of Lewis, by Caledonian MacBrayne. At the same time the ferry from Mallaig and Kyle

Macrae & Dick operated DST 365 an Austin K4 LV with Churchill 30 seat body. New in 1949 it passed to Highland in 1952 and was withdrawn in 1957. (ABC)

Number ST 8667, an Albion-bodied Albion PK114 of Macrae & Dick is in Strothers Lane. Built in 1936 it was withdrawn by Highland in 1953. (OS)

AV 7256 a 1935 Albion PW69 with Walker B34F body is parked outside the garage in Strothers Lane. It passed from Macrae & Dick to Highland in 1952 and was not withdrawn until 1956. (ABC)

of Lochalsh to Stornaway was withdrawn, a move not appreciated at Mallaig. The twice weekly bus service from Ullapool to Inverness was altered to be twice daily on weekdays with additional journeys on Mondays, Saturdays and summer Fridays. To cope with the increased loadings four Alexander Y type-bodied Leyland Leopards were acquired, these were the first new heavyweight coaches to be bought by Highland for a number of years.

In the summer of 1973 Highland announced its intention to withdraw all services on the Isle of Islay in favour of post buses. The date of transfer was 1st October when three Commer post buses took over the services from Portnahaven to Port Ellen and Port Askaig to Port Ellen.

It was announced in 1974 that a new overhaul works would be built at Seafield Road to replace the cramped works at Needlefield, Longman Road which had been inherited from Highland Transport and part of which had been Alexander's depot prior to their purchase of Grieg's. The new central works opened in October 1975. Changes were also planned for Fort William where a new bus station and rail terminal were to be built at the north eastern end of the town, the existing stations being in the way of a new relief road for the High Street which would run along the shore of Loch Linnhe. British Railways started to use the new station on 2nd June 1975.

Continuing to pursue a policy of abandoning its remote outposts, Highland applied to withdraw the Tarbert to Maruig service on the Isle of Harris and on 1st December 1975 disposed of its Harris operation to Harris Garage Company. Isle of Mull services were transferred to R Bowman, Craignure on 4th April 1976. Skye was now the only island with services operated by Highland. The Arisaig to Mallaig service was taken over by Morar Motors limited on a short term licence from 12th July 1976 and the Post Office took over the Achnasheen to Laide service.

Major alterations were made to the Inverness town services on 30th May 1976, partly as a result of a new traffic management scheme with one-way streets. A new pattern of cross town services was introduced as well as a circular route. With one exception, the new services did not use Farraline Park bus station and this provided much needed relief for the space available. Deregulation of express services in 1980 brought some competition from other operators, resulting in a new approach to some services, notably Glasgow to Inverness. In July 1982 the Kessock Bridge was opened, replacing the ferry. This new routing of the A9 enabled journey times to the north to be reduced and several service revisions made. Dingwall depot closed at this time and operations transferred to Inverness and Tain.

The 1985 Transport Act brought in deregulation of stage services in the hope of cutting costs and thereby the subsidies needed to maintain services. It also paved the way for the sale of the state owned operators to the private sector. To prepare for this the Scottish Bus Group redrew some of its boundaries, creating smaller, more manageable units. These changes were made on 17th June 1985 when Highland handed over the Oban depot and seventeen vehicles to Midland Scottish, the successor to W Alexander & Sons (Midland) Ltd. This left Highland with a smaller operating area which it was hoped would make it more appealing to a management buy-out. In May 1988 a group of drivers at Inverness depot decided to launch their own business and compete with Highland on the town services with a fleet of minibuses under the name of Inverness Traction. Highland stepped up their services to meet this competition using minibuses with the Highland Terrier fleetname.

Inverness Traction continues to operate most of the town services and is now part of Stagecoach Bluebird, the buyer of Northern Scottish, formerly W Alexander & Sons (Northern) Ltd. In 1990 the Highland Scottish fleet name was dropped in favour of Highland Bus & Coach and in August 1991 was sold by the Scottish Bus Group to a consortium of Clansman Travel and Rapsons. Highland Country being the fleet name adopted for most of the stage services.

Croft had built the body on this Commer Commando which had been new to Macrae and Dick, becoming No. L126 in the Highland fleet in 1952. It is in Nairn bus station about to depart for Inverness via Cawdor and Culloden. In the background can be seen former No. 170 now serving as the bus station café.

Parked in Academy Street awaiting departure for Fort George via Dalcross is CST 256 Leyland-bodied PD1 new in 1948 to Wemyss Bros. of Ardersier. This passed to Alexanders in 1950 and then to Highland in 1952. (OS)

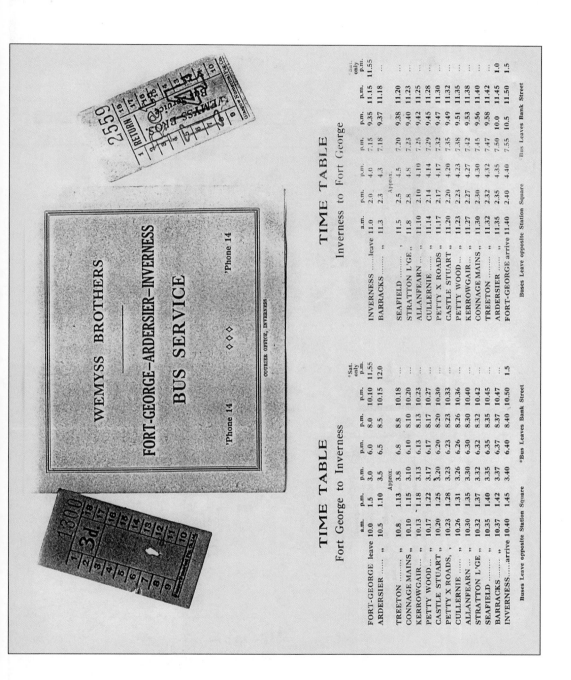

WEMYSS BROTHERS

FORT-GEORGE—ARDERSIER—INVERNESS

BUS SERVICE

'Phone 14 ◇◇◇ 'Phone 14

COURIER OFFICE, INVERNESS.

TIME TABLE
Fort George to Inverness

	a.m.	p.m.	p.m.	p.m.	p.m.	p.m.	*Sat. only p.m.
FORT-GEORGE leave	10.0	1.5	3.0	6.0	8.0	10.10	11.55
ARDERSIER "	10.5	1.10	3.5	6.5	8.5	10.15	12.0
			Approx.				
TREETON "	10.8	1.13	3.8	6.8	8.8	10.18	...
CONNAGE MAINS "	10.10	1.15	3.10	6.10	8.10	10.20	...
KERROWGAIR "	10.13	1.18	3.13	6.13	8.13	10.23	...
PETTY WOOD "	10.17	1.22	3.17	6.17	8.17	10.27	...
CASTLE STUART "	10.20	1.25	3.20	6.20	8.20	10.30	...
PETTY X ROADS,	10.23	1.28	3.23	6.23	8.23	10.33	...
CULLERNIE "	10.26	1.31	3.26	6.26	8.26	10.36	...
ALLANFEARN "	10.30	1.35	3.30	6.30	8.30	10.40	...
STRATTON L'GE "	10.32	1.37	3.32	6.32	8.32	10.42	...
SEAFIELD "	10.35	1.40	3.35	6.35	8.35	10.45	...
BARRACKS "	10.37	1.42	3.37	6.37	8.37	10.47	...
INVERNESS arrive	10.40	1.45	3.40	6.40	8.40	10.50	1.5

Buses Leave opposite Station Square   *Bus Leaves Bank Street

TIME TABLE
Inverness to Fort George

	a.m.	p.m.	p.m.	p.m.	p.m.	p.m.	Sat. only p.m.
INVERNESS leave	11.0	2.0	4.0	7.15	9.35	11.15	11.55
BARRACKS "	11.3	2.3	4.3	7.18	9.37	11.18	...
			Approx.				
SEAFIELD ,	11.5	2.5	4.5	7.20	9.38	11.20	...
STRATTON L'GE "	11.8	2.8	4.8	7.23	9.40	11.23	...
ALLANFEARN "	11.10	2.10	4.10	7.25	9.42	11.25	...
CULLERNIE "	11.14	2.14	4.14	7.29	9.45	11.28	...
PETTY X ROADS "	11.17	2.17	4.17	7.32	9.47	11.30	...
CASTLE STUART "	11.20	2.20	4.20	7.35	9.49	11.32	...
PETTY WOOD "	11.23	2.23	4.23	7.38	9.51	11.35	...
KERROWGAIR "	11.27	2.27	4.27	7.42	9.53	11.38	...
CONNAGE MAINS "	11.30	2.30	4.30	7.45	9.56	11.40	...
TREETON "	11.32	2.32	4.32	7.47	9.58	11.42	...
ARDERSIER "	11.35	2.35	4.35	7.50	10.0	11.45	1.0
FORT-GEORGE arrive	11.40	2.40	4.40	7.55	10.5	11.50	1.5

Buses Leave opposite Station Square   Bus Leaves Bank Street

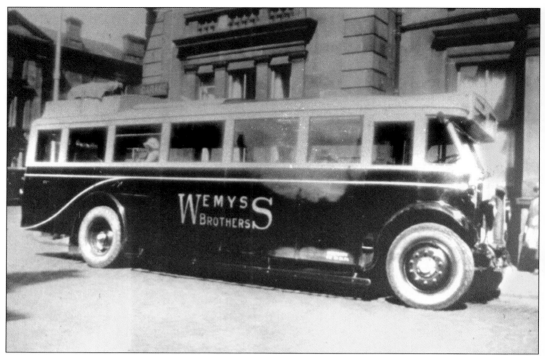

Number MS 9191, a Leyland LT1 with Alexander body was new in 1929 to Alexanders and joined the Wemyss fleet in 1935.

This wartime view is of Greig's Leyland TD1 WE 8780 working in London on loan. The London Transport fleetnumber plate can be seen on the waistband of the emergency door immediately behind the driver's cab.

Greig's VD 1753, an Albion, is parked on Bank Street for departure to Culduthel.

Greig's CK 4226 an Leyland-bodied Leyland TD2 is in Academy Street and shows an Alexander's fleetnumber, R561 after the sale in December 1947. (OS)

ROUTE No. 9—ACADEMY STREET TO INFIRMARY.

TUESDAY, THURSDAY, SATURDAY.

		p.m.
Academy Street	.... dep.	2 50
Infirmary	.... arr.	3 0

		p.m.
Infirmary	.... dep.	4 5
Academy Street	.... arr.	4 10

FARE—3d Single.

ROUTE No. 10—ACADEMY STREET TO DOCHFOUR DRIVE
VIA BRUCE GARDENS.

		p.m.	p.m.	p.m.	p.m.	p.m.	p.m.	p.m.
Academy Street	.... dep.	12 55	1 55	2 55	3 55	4 55	5 55	6 55
Park Road	.... ,,	1 0	2 0	3 0	4 0	5 0	6 0	7 0
Columba Road	...... ,,	1 3	2 3	3 3	4 3	5 3	6 3	7 3
Dochfour Drive	..... arr.	1 4	2 4	3 4	4 4	5 4	6 4	7 4

		p.m.	p.m.	p.m.	p.m.	p.m.	p.m.	p.m.
Dochfour Drive	..... dep.	1 5	2 5	3 5	4 5	5 5	6 5	7 5
Park Road	.... ,,	1 9	2 9	3 9	4 9	5 9	6 9	7 9
Academy Street	.... arr.	1 15	2 15	3 15	4 15	5 15	6 15	7 15

FARES—Academy Street to Park Road, 1d; to Dochfour Drive, 2d.

In February 1952 Inverness Town Services were transferred from W Alexander & Sons to Highland
Omnibuses, along with some vehicles. This Leyland was a 1935 TS7 which had been rebuilt to TD4
standards and fitted with an Alexander body in 1943. Number J153 is still in Alexander livery when
seen in September 1952. (ABC)

This view of No. E72 shows the emergency exit fitted immediately behind the cab door. The rear platform was later modified to incorporate an emergency exit.

Number E72 was exhibited at the 1951 Commercial Motor Show. This Guy Arab III has a lowbridge Strachan body and whilst striking in appearance was not popular with the drivers due to the problems of cab windows misting up in damp weather. It is waiting in Academy Street, Inverness for its departure to Nairn via Fort George.

High in the Cairngorm ski area is No. K90, its Strachan body proving useful for the carriage of skis as it had the emergency exit in the centre of the rear panel, in line with the gangway.

Alexander-bodied Leyland No. J160 was also originally a TS7 rebuilt to TD4 standards in 1944. It was transferred from W Alexander & Sons and had been repainted into Highland livery when seen in Farraline Park. (IMc)

Another Leyland rebuild to come from W Alexander & Sons was No. J155. It was originally a TS7 in the fleet of Simpson & Forrest of Dunfermline and passed to Alexanders in 1938. It was rebuilt as a TD4 and rebodied by Alexanders in 1943. (AI)

This Leyland TD1 with Croft body was new to Sheffield Corporation in 1930 and before joining the Highland fleet in 1952 as No. J162 had served with Paisley & District, Blair & Palmer of Carlisle, W Greig of Inverness and then W Alexander & Sons. Still in Alexander livery but with Highland fleetname, it is seen in Academy Street outside Inverness railway station. (OS)

Number J164 was new to Chesterfield Corporation in 1937 and this Leyland TD4 with MCCW body passed to W Alexander & Sons before joining the Highland fleet in 1952. (ABC)

Waiting at the Kessock Ferry, No. J164 shows evidence of some re-panelling. It was not popular with drivers as the sunken upper gangway continued to the front above the driver's cab. (IMc)

Another Leyland which had been new to Ribble was No. J165, a TD4 with Leyland body which was acquired from W Alexander & Sons with the Inverness town services. Photographed outside Wick depot it was used for carrying construction workers to Dounreay.

A more modern looking Leyland body is on this 1937 TD4, No. J167, which also came from Chesterfield Corporation via W Alexander & Sons.

Number J169 was new to Wemyss Brothers, Ardersier in 1948. This Leyland-bodied PD1 passed with the business to W Alexander & Sons and then to Highland in 1952. (ABC)

Farraline Park is the location for this view of J169, an all-Leyland PD1 which had been new to Wemyss Brothers of Ardersier. The vehicle alongside is E44, a Guy Arab I with Brush body.

Vehicles of The Highland Transport Company Limited

The strong winds which batter the Pentland Firth have caused No. J168 to partly overturn and it is seen with ropes attached to prevent it going completely on to its side on the 27th October 1955 at Clardon.

The first vehicles in the fleet of the Highland Transport Company Limited were those taken over from Inverness and District Motor Services in April 1930. The most popular make was Albion, some of which appear to have been purchased new. These eighteen vehicles continued in service until the 1940s. Highland Transport purchased some new vehicles in 1930, six more Albions and four AEC Regals, one of which had 14 seat coachwork of unknown origin for service on Skye and later passed to Nicolson (Skye Transport Company) in March 1935. The acquisition of the Portree Coach Company in August 1930 brought four more 14 seaters and an assortment of cars.

The first double deck bus was bought in 1931, an AEC Regent/Strachan H26/24R which had been a demonstrator. It was given fleet number 7 and was withdrawn in 1942. An Albion PMA28 was also purchased new that year and was followed in 1932 by two more Albions of different types. This period saw many vehicles taken into stock with the businesses purchased. The next two vehicles bought by Highland Transport new were in 1933, an AEC Regal and a Ford. The AEC Regal (No. 55) was later fitted with an oil engine and was not withdrawn until 1954. That same year saw the arrival of another AEC Regal, a former demonstrator, new the previous year. Numbered 54, its original body was replaced with the Cowieson body from the Gilford 'gas-bus' and also survived until 1954. Another demonstrator taken into stock that year was an Albion PW65 which remained on hire from Albion Motors until finally being purchased in January 1936. Five more Albion buses and a Ford coach were bought in 1935/6 and a second-hand Albion was purchased from Hebble Motor Services Limited of Halifax. New vehicles for 1937 were two more Albions,

49

This Bedford WTB with Duple C20F body was new to W Alexander & Sons in 1936 and passed to Highland in 1952. Number C172 originally had a canvas roof cover and is seen in Farraline Park, Inverness.

Number E89, another former London Transport Park Royal-bodied Guy Arab, is about to leave Farraline Park on the Culduthel service. This bus and No. E87 were withdrawn in 1954 and their chassis rebuilt for bodying as single deckers.

Not yet displaying its fleet number K75, this Guy Arab has been rebuilt by Scottish Omnibuses from a London Transport double decker. It is seen when new in Strothers Lane, Inverness before being put to work in the Caithness area. (ABC)

This Commer Commando with Scottish Aviation body was new to W Alexander & Sons of Falkirk in 1947 and passed to Highland in 1952. This 29 seater coach, No. L5 is about to leave Farraline Park for Holm Mills. After being withdrawn in 1961 it passed to Norman Smith of Grantown on Spey.

Leyland-bodied TS7 had been new in 1937 to Central SMT and came to Highland in 1955 The original Leyland body had been rebuilt by ECW in 1951. Number H6 is loading for the Nairn via Cawdor service. (IMc)

The double-deck style rear platform, often known as the Scottish doorway, can be seen clearly in this view of No. H7.

Number K95 was also rebuilt from a London Transport double-decker into a coach by Scottish Omnibuses. AEC mudguards and bonnet cover have been used in this conversion. It is seen in Glasgow on a Private Hire duty. (IMc)

the Gilford 'gas-bus' and a Rolls Royce 7 seat limousine. This had been new in 1926 but was rebuilt and re-registered in 1937. Cowieson-bodied Albions were again the choice for 1938 when four were bought, the rear entrance buses being rebuilt to forward entrance by Highland Transport; all were transferred to Highland Omnibuses. No. 79 was unusual in being a six-wheeler and was not withdrawn until 1957. Only two new buses arrived in 1939, a Bedford WTB and another Albion with Cowieson body.

In 1940 a small capacity bus was acquired from SMT Edinburgh, this being an Albion PH49/Cowieson B20F which had been new in 1933. Another second-hand purchase was of a Leyland TS2/Weymann from Wemyss Brothers of Ardersier. This had been new in 1931 to Scout Motor Services of Preston. It had also seen service with Elgin and District Motor Company Limited (Grey Line) as No. 21 and then P293 in the fleet of W Alexander & Sons Ltd, Falkirk, before passing to a London dealer. Central SMT supplied a Leyland TS7T/Leyland B38R and a Cowieson-bodied Albion PV70 coach that same year. Only one vehicle was bought in 1941 and this was through the Ministry of Transport for the War Department, who

sourced an Albion PW65/Alexander B36F formerly in the fleet of W Alexander & Sons Ltd, Falkirk. Numbered 99 it was not withdrawn until 1956. Six new vehicles were bought in 1942, three Bedford OWBs with SMT bodies, a Leyland TS11 and a Tillings-Stevens both with Willowbrook bodies and a Duple-bodied Albion CX9.

These were followed in 1943 by three more SMT-bodied Bedford OWBs and another three in 1944 but this time with Duple bodies. Two new double-deckers arrived in 1944 being Northern Counties lowbridge-bodied Guy Arab IIs. The final new war-time purchases came in 1945 with two more Duple-bodied Bedford OWBs and four lowbridge Guy Arab IIs, two each bodied by Weymann and Roe. Second-hand purchases that year were two Albion PW65s from W Alexander & Sons, Falkirk. These dated from 1933 and one was withdrawn later the same year and the other in 1952.

Eight new double-deckers were delivered in 1946 and were Guy Arab IIs with Strachan lowbridge bodies, also acquired was a Duple-bodied Bedford OWB from Wilson (Royal Hotel) Thurso which had been new in 1944 and used to carry service personnel to Scrabster pier. The Guy Arab

Roe-bodied Guy Arab II, No. E11 had been new to Scottish Omnibuses in 1944 and was transferred to Highland in 1955. It is ready to leave Inverness for the 85 mile journey to Helmsdale. It was to become a regular on the Dounreay contract until being withdrawn in 1963 and returned to work for three months with Scottish Omnibuses in Edinburgh. (IMc)

Roe-bodied Guy Arab II, E17 also went to work in the capital and is parked in St Andrew's Square bus station. It had been new to the David Lawson fleet in 1943.

A Duple-bodied Bedford OB? Well not quite, as this example was built at Marine Works by Scottish Omnibuses to the Duple design. The main differences being that the door slid back on the inside and the pointed corners to the destination screens. No. C23 had been new to Scottish Omnibuses in 1948 and moved to Highland in 1956, where it is seen waiting to take up its tour duty. It was withdrawn in 1961.

The first Albion Nimbus with Alexander C29F body, one of six supplied in 1956 is seen exhibited in St Andrews Square bus station in Edinburgh. The mainly cream livery was soon to be changed to red with cream window surrounds and waistband. (PJR)

Albion Nimbus No. A4 now in the revised livery is on a day tour to Loch Maree and is parked in a hotel grounds for a refreshment break. (IMc)

This AEC Monocoach with Alexander dual-purpose body is also on show in Edinburgh. Number B2 has its destination screen set for John O'Groats probably to show the extent of the Highland territory. (PJR)

Ten AEC Reliances were delivered in 1957 with Park Royal dual-purpose bodies. At Dingwall depot is No. B10 when new. (IMc)

was proving a popular vehicle and in 1947 seven more arrived, two more Arab IIs with Northern Counties bodies and five single-deckers, Arab IIIs two of which carried Guy bodies and the others were bodied by Strachan. Nineteen Forthy-Eight deliveries comprised two Guy Arab II/Northern Counties double-deckers and two Guy Arab III/Strachan single-deckers of which No. 67 was fitted in 1955 with a second-hand Alexander coach body.

The only new arrivals in 1949 were two more Strachan-bodied Guy Arab III single deckers. These were both to receive second-hand Alexander bodies, No. 86 with a bus body in 1955 and No. 83 a coach body in 1958. The three 1950 Guy Arab single-deckers were again bodied by Strachan and were not rebodied but extensively refurbished in 1960.

A notable purchase in 1951 was a Guy Arab III which had been exhibited at the 1950 Commercial Motor Show. This had a fully-fronted Strachan lowbridge body and took the fleet number 72. It spent most of its life working from Inverness on the Nairn via Fort George service before being transferred to Thurso for the two years before its withdrawal in 1970. It then travelled further

north to serve for two years with JD Pearce in Orkney. The last vehicles purchased by Highland Transport Company were another three Guy Arab single deckers which carried Strachan bodies and remained in service until 1968 and 1969. In November 1951 Macrae & Dick was bought by the BTC and twenty three single-deckers passed to Highland Transport, mainly Albions and Bedfords but also four Austins, a Commer Commando and a Leyland TS7.

Northern Counties-bodied Guy Arab II of 1943, No. E5, came from Western SMT in 1957 and is seen in Needlefield garage after having adverts painted on to its sides. The Albion Nimbus in the background is having a full repaint. (IMc)

Brush had built the body on this Guy Arab I No. E40, which came from Scottish Omnibuses in 1958 after a rebuild at Marine Works. It was mainly used on Inverness town services.

Vehicles of Highland Omnibuses Limited

The first deliveries to the new Highland Omnibuses Limited were six Guy Arabs which had been new to London Transport as double-deckers but had been rebuilt with new single deck bodies and the chassis lengthened to thirty feet by Scottish Omnibuses Limited. These buses gained the nickname of 'kangaroos' due to the way that their rear ends bounced around when running empty or with only a few passengers. Twelve more such rebuilds entered the fleet in the following two years, of which six had coach bodies and were used on tours and Private Hire duties. Two more ex-London Transport Guy Arabs were taken into stock but only lasted a couple of years before going to SMT to be rebuilt into new single-deckers. Scottish Omnibuses also supplied another ex-London Transport Guy Arab and a Kenex-bodied Austin CXD coach, the Arab returning south in 1954 for reconstruction as a single decker. In 1953 W Alexander & Sons Ltd of Falkirk supplied six Commer Commando coaches with bodywork by Scottish Aviation and these were followed in December by two Leyland TS8s from Central SMT. These had Alexander rear entrance bodies which looked unusual in the Highland fleet as they had open rear platforms as found on double-deckers. This type of entrance was not uncommon in the south of Scotland. In 1955 Highland received the prototype Albion Nimbus with SMT bodywork for evaluation purposes. This vehicle was returned to Albion Motors in 1956 when six Alexander coach-bodied Albion Nimbuses were delivered. These were not well liked by drivers as they were regarded as underpowered. More second-hand vehicles arrived in 1956 to cope with the expansion at Thurso with the construction of Dounreay. There were two more Commer Commando coaches from Alexanders and three from David Lawson who also supplied ten Guy Arabs with bodies by Duple, Strachan, Roe and Northern Counties. Later in the year

Scottish Omnibuses supplied another Guy Arab and six Bedford OB coaches.

Nineteen Fifty-Seven brought the first underfloor-engined AECs into the fleet with the delivery of six Monocoaches and six Reliances with Park Royal dual-purpose bodies which were based at Inverness and Thurso although Dornoch and Dingwall each received a Reliance. Most of these vehicles were to remain in service for fifteen years. The popular Guy Arab continued to arrive in quantity from David Lawson, Western SMT and Scottish Omnibuses who also supplied another Bedford OB coach. Another four dual-purpose Reliances arrived in 1958 along with seven more Guy Arabs which had been refurbished by Scottish Omnibuses. January 1959 brought Alexander dual purpose bodied Reliances which for the first few years were used on Private Hires and coach duties. Secondhand acquisitions were seven Bedford SBs with Burlingham coach bodies and another two Guy Arabs, one bodied by Brush and the other by Northern Counties. With the approach of winter there was a demand from the Caithness area for double-deckers with platform doors and some Guy Arabs from the Inverness area were sent to Scottish Omnibuses to have doors fitted. In the absence of these vehicles, Highland hired four AEC Monocoaches from Scottish Omnibuses. When the Guys returned they were sent to Caithness in exchange for open platform buses which returned to Inverness. March 1960 brought another five Alexander-bodied AEC Reliances which were dual-purpose vehicles and were delivered in an all cream livery with red window surrounds and waistband. Within two years they were repainted mainly red with cream roof and waistbands. Two more Guy Arabs were acquired the following month from Western SMT. These had Eastern Coach Works bodies already fitted with platform doors and were allocated to the Caithness area where they served until 1965. The only other arrival that year was another Burlingham-bodied

Former Western SMT Guy Arab II was new in 1943 with a Northern Counties body. It was rebodied by ECW in 1951 and passed to Highland in 1960. No. E67 was based at Wick depot from where it is shown operating the Dunbeath service. (AJD)

Guy Arab II, No. E41 had its Weymann body totally rebuilt by Scottish Omnibuses before joining the Highland fleet in 1958 where it received further body refurbishment including the fitting of platform doors in 1963. It is seen turning into Dingwall depot. (AJD)

Number B36, GSC 457, is an AEC Regal III with Burlingham FC35F body and is seen in Dingwall on route 17 to Inverness. It was acquired from Scottish Omnibuses in 1962 and withdrawn in 1963. It was not popular with crews because of its full-front style and also being 8ft wide. (GW)

Number D1 an AEC Regent III with Northern Counties body was new to Western SMT in 1947 and entered the Highland fleet in January 1963. It was Highland's first air-braked double-decker and had a 9.6 litre engine with pre-selective transmission. It is awaiting departure for Nairn via Fort George from Farraline Park.

Academy Street, Inverness is the location of D2. This Daimler CWA6 was supplied new to James Sutherland of Peterhead with Duple L27/26RD body. It passed with that business to W Alexander & Sons Ltd in 1950 who had the doors removed. It entered the Highland fleet in January 1964 and was withdrawn in December of that year.

Parked at the remote village of Bettyhill on the north coast is Albion Victor, A7, with Duple C31F body. It had been operated by three previous owners, passing to Highland with the business of John Bain & Sons of North Erradale, Gairloch. (GW)

Bedford SB coach from Scottish Omnibuses. New for 1961 were six AEC Reliances with Alexander C38F bodies which had glass front domes and cove panels. These were painted in the red and cream coach livery and later received the grey and blue coach livery introduced in 1968. They ended their days on the Dounreay contracts after being reclassified as buses. More second-hand coaches came in 1961 from Scottish Omnibuses, twelve Burlingham-bodied Bedford OBs and two Duple-bodied AEC Regals. These extra coaches were needed to cope with the increasing popularity of touring holidays in the north. Delivered in May 1962 were six Alexander-bodied AEC Reliances identical to those new the previous year. Scottish Omnibuses again supplied more coaches, six Duple-bodied AEC Regals, six Bedford SBs with Burlingham bodywork and one Burlingham-bodied AEC Regal which was not a popular vehicle and was withdrawn after one year.

A large intake of vehicles from Western SMT came in 1963 which included thirteen coaches with Alexander bodies built on Guy Arab UF chassis which earned the nickname 'bombers'. There was also an AEC Regent with Northern Counties body and two Guy Arabs with Alexander bodies fitted with platform doors. The most significant arrival of 1963 was when twelve Bristol Lodekkas arrived to take up duties on the Inverness town services. These had been new to Scottish Omnibuses seven years earlier and brought to Inverness the benefits of a single step entrance to the lower saloon and removed the inconvenient side gangway from the upper saloon. Drivers had to adjust to a five speed gearbox and the fact that these buses were eight feet in width. Three more second-hand Guy Arabs arrived including, unusually, a highbridge type which was considered a liability for Inverness and was sent up to Thurso where it did not last long as it did not have platform doors. A new chassis type entered the fleet in 1964 with the arrival of eight diesel-engined Bedford VAS1s with dual-purpose bodies by Duple Midland, two of which were later rebuilt to include a mail compartment. Vehicles from

the fleets of Ross of Balblair, MacKenzie of Garve and MacKintosh of Croy joined the Highland fleet when these businesses were taken over in 1964. W Alexander (Midland) supplied an all-Leyland TD7 and three Daimler CWA6s, two with Duple bodies and one with Brush bodywork. Central SMT supplied five Guy Arab UF coaches with Alexander bodies, three similar coaches came from Western SMT along with three Alexander-bodied Daimler CVG6s and seven AEC Regal IVs with Alexander bus bodies, one of which was fitted out as a dual-purpose vehicle. Scottish Omnibuses sent two more Burlingham-bodied AEC Regal III coaches and four Ford 570Es with coach bodies by Duple Northern which had been new in 1962/3. Two new dual purpose vehicles arrived early in 1965 which again were Bedford VAS1s bodied by Duple Midland and in March the vehicles and services of the Achnasheen Hotel Company were taken over. They operated mainly around Wester Ross and combined a goods and mail service to the more remote parts.

The following month Scottish Omnibuses again provided two Burlingham-bodied AEC Regal coaches for the Caithness area. Albions once again entered the fleet in May with the arrival of four Alexander-bodied Lowlanders, these were the first forward entrance double-deckers in the Highland fleet. Four more similar vehicles arrived in July and another four in December, these last four having bodywork by Northern Counties of Wigan. All had been new to Central SMT and were quickly sent to Thurso to work on the Dounreay services where they replaced some of the Guy Arabs.

An assortment of second-hand coaches arrived from Alexander Midland in July, four Daimler CVD6s with ECW FC37F bodies, two Albion NS3Ls with Alexander bodies and a Guy Arab with Duple body. Between September and December twenty-two Guy Arab UFs with centre entrance Alexander coach bodies made their way north from Western SMT. The October acquisition of Fred Newton, Dingwall brought more vehicles into the fleet although not all were to enter service.

On Dores Road on Route 3 to Holm Mills is J1, an all Leyland TD7 new to W Alexander & Sons Ltd in 1940. It passed to Highland in January 1964 and was withdrawn later that year. (GW)

A rear view of vehicles at the stances in Farraline Park bus station. On the left is K2, a Guy Arab UF with Alexander C30CT body; in the middle is E51, a Guy Arab II with Northern Counties body, new to Highland Transport Company in 1946, and on the right is C27, a Bedford SB with Burlingham C30F body new to Scottish Omnibuses in 1952.

New in 1966 was a small coach with a goods and mail compartment that had been exhibited at the Scottish Motor Show at Kelvin Hall the previous November. This was a Bedford VAM5 with Alexander C24FM body which was used on the Thurso – Bettyhill – Tongue route. Two vehicles were diverted from Simpson of Rosehearty when that firm was taken over by Alexander Northern. One was a Ford R226 with a Plaxton coach body and the other a Ford R192 with Duple Midland bus bodywork. The bus was used on an Inverness town service to the Raigmore estate and was one of the first one man operated vehicles on town services. Another Scottish Show exhibit, from 1961, arrived in April and this was a prototype Albion Lowlander with Alexander body from Western SMT and over the next few months a further eleven with Northern Counties bodies arrived. In March a Ford 570E coach was purchased from Happiways tours of Manchester who had operated in an all grey livery with dark blue band. Highland decided to adopt this livery for their coach fleet and gradually vehicles were repainted from the red and cream. Another Ford 570E was bought from Loch Lomond Coaches which also arrived in grey livery. The business of NR Smith of Grantown on Spey was taken over in December with an assortment of vehicles, some of which had previously served in the Highland fleet. Very few of these vehicles were retained by Highland for continued service. Three coaches were taken into stock with the purchase in May 1967 of S MacGregor of Dornoch and in the same month six new Alexander-bodied Bedford VAM5s were delivered, painted in the new grey and blue coach livery. They were used on summer tours and then fitted out for one man operation and allocated to Nairn depot for the winter. Mail services on the north coast were acquired with Peter Burr (Omnibuses) Limited of Tongue in June. Two vehicles were taken over but only one continued in service. The purchase in August of Robertson, Strathglass brought two more vehicles and again only one was to stay in the Highland fleet. The next source of used vehicles was Red and White Services of Chepstow who provided six Guy Arab UF coaches with Duple bodies.

John Bain & Son of North Erradale, near Gairloch operatred this Spurling-bodied Bedford mail bus EJS 725, which is shown amongst typical West Coast scenery. This vehicle had been replaced before the business was sold to Highland in 1964.

New to MacKenzie, Garve, Kenex 11 seat bodywork is fitted to this Morris J2VM supplied in 1959. FJS 254 has become M2 in the Highland fleet and is seen in typical Wester Ross coastal scenery.

At Garve Post Office on its journey to the West is FGS 872, a Bedford A4LB9 with Duple body, which had been modified to become a Mail bus. It belonged to the Achnasheen Hotel Company.

Number K22 had been exhibited at Earl's Court in 1952. It was a Guy Arab UF with Alexander body. It was the only vehicle to receive this style of body with sliding door, glass louvers over the windows and curved glass roof windows. Delivered to Western SMT in 1953 it passed to Highland in 1965. (GW)

These were converted for driver only operation and used to replace buses taken over from N Smith in the Spey valley. The need for more vehicles suitable for one man operation was satisfied by the purchase from Ribble of six Leyland Royal Tigers with Leyland 44 seat bus bodies. These were eventually used on the ski services in the Cairngorms, the emergency door in the centre of the rear being ideal for the loading of skis. One bus was adapted by Alexander Coachworks by moving the rear bulkhead forward and creating an open platform for the stowage of 24 sets of skis. Another twenty nine vehicles were brought into the Highland fleet in 1967 from other Scottish group companies. Western SMT supplied the double-deckers which were two Leyland PD1s, five Leyland PD2s, three Guy Arabs and six Albion Lowlanders. Alexander Midland and Fife each supplied three Alexander-bodied Leyland PS1 coaches and Alexander Northern supplied four Ford 570Es and three Bedford SB1s all with Duple coachwork, which were quickly fitted out for one man operation by the addition of destination screens and a long lever at the right hand side of the driver's seat to operate the sliding door. Although

fitted for bus use they were painted in the new coach livery.

New vehicles arrived in the spring of 1968 and comprised six Bedford VAS5s with dual-purpose Willowbrook bodies painted in the red and green livery, six Bedford VAM70s also with dual-purpose Willowbrook bodies but painted in blue and grey and two Ford R192s with Willowbrook bus bodies which introduced a new livery style of red for the roof, window surrounds and a broad band in the middle of the side panels and the remainder of the vehicle painted light cream. Two more similar Fords arrived in September and enabled more services to be converted to one man operation. Second-hand acquisitions were a Ford 570E with Duple coachwork and a Ford R192 with Duple Northern body from Alexander Fife. An ex-Government Karrier with 14 seat Strachan body was bought for use in the Diabeg area of Wester Ross. Twenty five Guy Arab LUFs with Alexander bodywork came from Western SMT in July and displaced some earlier centre-entrance coaches which were unsuitable for one man operation.

Twelve new arrivals in 1969 were Willowbrook bus bodied Ford R192s,

AJS 893B is now MB1 in the Highland fleet. It is a Harrington-bodied Commer 1500LBD. Seen at Needlefield Garage, it came to Highland with the business of Fred Newton, Dingwall.

A rear view of the Bedford OB number SO 9111 operating for Norman Smith, Grantown on Spey.

Robertson of Strathglass sold out to Highland in 1967. ST 8578 Albion BL119 with Stewart FB14FM body was new in 1936 and withdrawn in 1952.

UNK 229, this 1955 Bedford SBG of Robertson of Strathglass carries a Thurgood body. It passed to Highland in 1967 and was withdrawn the following year.

sixteen Alexander-bodied AEC Reliance coaches from Scottish Omnibuses and from Central SMT came two Leyland PD2s with Northern Counties bodies and six Bristol Lodekkas. In 1970 further new vehicles were twelve new Ford R192s with Willowbrook bus bodies and one Bedford SB5 also with Willowbrook body which was originally ordered by David MacBrayne. The Highland fleet then expanded massively with the takeover of the David MacBrayne services and also the Oban depot of Alexander Midland. It was at this time that a new livery was introduced of peacock blue and poppy red which was to last for the next ten years. No new vehicles were delivered early in 1971 but Western SMT supplied two Bristol RELH coaches with Alexander bodies which were used on express services and another twelve Albion Lowlanders, seven with Alexander bodies and five built by Northern Counties. These were different from earlier Lowlanders in having manual gearboxes and air suspension and were at first on loan, being officially acquired in January 1972. Late in the year another nine new Ford R192s arrived again with Willowbrook bus bodies. Early in 1972 seven dual-purpose Alexander-bodied Bristol LS6Gs arrived from Western SMT for use on one man operations but were not popular with drivers due to their age and fittings. In June and July another twelve Ford R192s arrived, all bodied by Willowbrook. Four of these were dual-purpose vehicles which were painted in the coach livery and the others had bus seats and received the red and peacock blue livery. Albion single deckers made a return to the fleet in February 1973 when six Vikings with Alexander coach bodies were transferred from Eastern Scottish. A new roll-on/roll-off ferry service to the Isle of Lewis was established from Ullapool early in 1973 which replaced the crane-loading service which operated from Mallaig and Kyle of Lochalsh. A connecting coach

Number E1 was originally a Northern Counties utility-bodied Guy Arab II new to London Transport in 1945. It was sold to Western SMT in 1954 who had it rebodied by Northern Counties with the 'new look' front. It passed to Highland in 1967 and was withdrawn the following year. (AJD)

service was needed to Inverness as the nearest railway station was at Garve some 32 miles away. To meet this need four Leyland Leopards with Alexander coach bodies were diverted from orders for other companies, one of these was rebodied in 1976 after being extensively damaged in an accident on the road from Inverness to Ullapool. A total of seventeen new Fords were delivered in 1973 including a Duple coach-bodied R1114, the remainder being Willowbrook-bodied R1014s with either bus or dual-purpose seating. Second-hand double-deckers were urgently needed as a result of gaining more school contracts and Eastern Scottish supplied a Leyland PD2, an AEC Renown, two Bridgemasters all with Park Royal bodies and another Lodekka. Alexander Midland provided another Albion Lowlander and Alexander Northern four Leyland PD2/12s with Alexander bodies and one PD2/20 with Northern Counties body. The Lowlander was the first to have an extended linkage to enable the crew to change the destination display without having to climb up on the bonnet. To improve safety it was decided to fit all Lowlanders with this equipment. More used coaches arrived, being six Alexander-bodied AEC Reliances from Eastern Scottish and five Duple-bodied Bedford VAMs from Central SMT.

A few unusual double-deckers arrived in 1974. Six Leyland PD3s with Alexander forward entrance bodies came from Edinburgh Corporation Transport, including PWS 998 which had the Homalloy glass-fibre front end and bonnet. These buses were highbridge and were given yellow plates with black fleetnumbers HB1-6 to highlight to drivers that fact. An Albion Lowlander LR7 was purchased from SM Ementon of Cranfield which had been new to Luton Corporation. This had an East Lancashire body with a sliding door which made it unique in the Highland fleet. Six more Ford R1114 coaches with 49 seat Alexander bodies arrived in July and were spread around the depots. Their blue and grey livery was later replaced by bus livery and some subsequently received all-over advertising. August brought ten Ford R1114s with Alexander bus bodies which were used to extend single manning and in some cases replace double-deckers. Another unusual purchase was from W Irvine of Law, this being a Strachan dual-purpose bodied Ford R226. The final arrivals in the fleet in 1974

McKintosh, Croy operated ST 7657, a 14 seat Ford T. It is seen in Strothers Lane shortly before withdrawal.

JS 8710, a Mulliner-bodied Bedford OB, waits in Academy Street. It is in the ownership of MacKenzie, Garve but had been withdrawn before the sale to Highland in 1964.

This line of Albion Lowlanders in Thurso depot shows the various body types and liveries in the early 1970s.

In 1967, three Leyland PS1 Alexander with C35F bodies came from the Alexander Fife fleet. J10 is still in Fife red livery at Farraline Park.

were two more Albion Lowlanders with Northern Counties bodywork, these came from Alexander Fife but had been new to Central SMT. Fifteen more Ford R1114s were delivered in the summer of 1975, the first six were coaches and the others buses all with Alexander bodies. More second-hand single-deckers arrived to cover vehicle shortages being six Alexander-bodied AEC Reliances from Alexander Northern which were operated for only two months in their yellow livery before being withdrawn and were not even allocated fleetnumbers. In November another two Albion Lowlanders were purchased from Alexander Midland which replaced some of the Edinburgh Leyland PD3s. During 1975 vehicles were hired from Western SMT to cover for late delivery of new buses at the height of the tourist season. These were two Leyland PD3s with Northern Counties L35/32RD bodies and two Bristol MWs with Alexander DP41F bodies. July 1965 also saw five Leyland Leopards on hire from Central SMT which were returned in mid August when they were needed for schools duties. An interesting double-decker was also hired and eventually purchased, this was another Albion Lowlander which received fleetnumber AL49. The chassis

had been supplied to Edinburgh Corporation Transport in 1962 but had never been bodied before being sold back to Albion in 1964. It was sold on to Western SMT and sent to Northern Counties for bodying in 1965 with other Lowlanders and so acquired a 1965 registration BCS 252C.

A familiar pattern followed in 1976 with new Fords and second-hand Lowlanders. The four Ford R1014s delivered in March and the six R1114s delivered in June had Duple Dominant coach bodies. T120, the first of the 49 seat R1114s was rebodied in October 1978 following an accident on the Ullapool service during the 1977 Christmas period. Four Albion Lowlanders with Alexander bodies were purchased from Alexander Midland. No less than thirty six new Ford R1114s were delivered between February and August 1977 of which fourteen were Duple Dominant coaches, twelve Duple Dominant buses and ten Alexander-bodied buses. Two of the Duple buses were reseated as coaches in April 1978 to increase coach availability; they were refitted with bus seats in November 1981. The last of the Alexander-bodied buses, T161, was fitted in 1981 with a mail compartment as B31FM layout to replace CD13 on the Thurso to Tongue route. Two

This line of buses in Thurso carries workers from Dounreay. BA3 leads the convoy and is an AEC Reliance with Alexander coach body.

small capacity coaches were acquired from Alexander Midland which became CD94/5, these being Bedford VAS5s with Duple Dominant C29F bodies. The first rear-engined double-deckers arrived in May with six Daimler Fleetlines with Alexander bodies from Alexander Fife. These were used for one man operation in Inverness on town services. In October an exchange was arranged with Alexander Northern which saw five Leyland Leopards going east and Highland gaining five Ford R1114s with Alexander coach bodies. In 1978 two coaches were acquired with the bus business of Greig's Garages (Inverness) Limited which were only used for a short time on occasional school duties. They were soon withdrawn and never allocated fleet numbers. In August it was the turn of Western SMT to supply six Daimler Fleetlines with Northern Counties bodywork. One of these was to have its roof removed by a low bridge on Friday 13th of November 1981 when returning to the depot. It was rebuilt and gave four more years service. The first new double-deckers to be delivered to Highland Omnibuses Limited arrived in October 1978. These were six Leyland Fleetline FE30AGRs with

Eastern Coach Works H43/32F bodies to the design normally associated with the Bristol VR. They replaced Albion Lowlanders enabling more Inverness town services to be converted to one man operation from 5th November. These were followed by nine identical vehicles in June 1979 of which four went to Thurso depot and were the first new double-deckers in Caithness for thirty years. June also saw delivery of two more Duple Dominant coaches on Ford R1114 chassis which were allocated to the Oban depot where they remained until transfer of Oban depot back to Alexander Midland in 1985. Another two similar coaches arrived in August and were followed by five Ford R1014s with Duple Dominant C45F bodies which had been new to Alexander Fife. In September an Alexander-bodied Fleetline was purchased for spares from Grampian Regional Transport.

The Leyland National had become the standard single-decker for the National Bus Company fleets but was not a common sight in Scotland. The first to join the Highland fleet were eight Series 2 models which arrived in June 1980 entering service on Inverness town routes. Four new coaches were Ford R1114s again with Duple

Number BA20 was taken over with the services of David MacBrayne and is outside Portree depot. This Willowbrook-bodied AEC Reliance had worked the express service from Glasgow to Uig pier.

Dominant bodywork. A new make of vehicle for Highland was the Ailsa, ten of which were received that year. These were Alexander-bodied full height buses and had been new to Alexander Fife in 1974 /5 and were soon to be despatched to Wick and Thurso depots where there were no low bridge problems. The Ailsa chassis was built at Irvine and combined a front entrance and front engine enabling one man operation without some of the problems associated with rear engines. Eleven Leyland Leopards with Alexander coach bodies were acquired from Western SMT in February 1981 and were followed in May by ten new Alexander-bodied Leopards which were for express duties. Four were based in Inverness, two at Portree, two at Fort William and two at Oban. The Oban pair were transferred to Alexander Midland and then to Oban & District, both still being in service in August 2005. Another Ailsa was acquired from Alexander Midland and joined the others in Caithness. Ten Daimler Fleetlines with Eastern Coach Works bodies were acquired from Alexander Fife in March as were seven Ford R1114s with Alexander bus bodies and these were followed by six Duple Dominant coaches on Leyland Leopard chassis. These six were later painted in

Scottish Citylink livery. To replace accident victim T98 a Ford R1114 with Alexander bus body was acquired from Alexander Midland. In November five Leyland Leopards with Alexander wide entrance bus bodies were purchased from Alexander Northern, two of which were modified to B62F format. Five new Leyland Leopards with Alexander B62F bodies were delivered in February 1982, the high capacity being useful on school services. Two more bus-bodied Leopards came from Alexander Midland and in September ten Leyland Leopards with Alexander coach bodies were acquired from Western SMT An unusual purchase in September was a Duple demonstrator, a Leyland Tiger with C49FT body which was used on Scottish Citylink routes and was painted in that livery in 1983. A Leyland Leopard was bought from Alexander Northern in January 1983 which had Alexander Motorway Express style of bodywork and was also repainted into Citylink livery. It was soon withdrawn after sustaining accident damage. In April there was a need for more double-deckers and this was met by the purchase of ten Eastern Coach Works-bodied Daimler Fleetlines from Eastern Scottish and two Alexander-bodied examples from Alexander Midland.

Standing in Farraline Park is CD75, a Willowbrook-bodied Bedford SB. It is about to work the country lane route to Foyers on the south side of Loch Ness.

Oban's famous landmark, McCaigs Tower, is prominent in this view of T59 working the cross town service from Mill Park to Kerrera Terrace. This Ford R192 with Willowbrook body is in the coach livery. (PTP)

Six Leyland Leopards with Duple Dominant bodies came from Alexander Fife in 1982. L245 is at Farraline Park.

Fort William was not allocated double-deckers until the early 1980s. D348, an ECW-bodied Daimler Fleetline, had been new to Central SMT and is seen on a town service.

Extra school contracts resulted in Highland buying two ex-London Transport DMSs from which the centre doors had been removed by Western SMT on their way north. D50 had MCW bodywork.

Number R999 in Scottish Citylink livery is in St Andrew's Square bus station, Edinburgh. This Volvo B10M with Van Hool body was new to Clydeside Scottish.

A return to ex-London Transport vehicles came in August when two MCW-bodied Daimler Fleetlines (MLH 440/1L) were bought from Western SMT, in the same month two large capacity Alexander-bodied Leopards were acquired from Alexander Fife. Before the year ended, fifteen Alexander-bodied Leyland Leopard coaches were purchased from Western SMT and many reseated as buses. New double-deckers returned to Highland in January 1984 with the purchase of six Leyland Olympians with Alexander bodywork. These were followed by five Leyland Atlanteans from Grampian Regional Transport which had their centre exits panelled over rather than removed. Four new Leyland Tigers with Duple Laser bodies were purchased for Citylink duties.

In February 1985 another nine new Olympians arrived and were shared between Inverness, Nairn and Tain. Another six Leyland Tigers with Duple Laser bodies followed of which four were in Citylink livery and the other two in an all grey coach livery. In April three Ford R1114s were exchanged for three Leyland Leopards with Alexander Midland in preparation for the transfer of the Oban

depot and duly returned to Midland in June 1985. Eight coaches and four double-deck buses were acquired with the business of Newton, Dingwall in December. Early in 1986 the two Volvo B10MT-53s included in the purchase were exchanged with two Leyland Tigers from Clydeside Scottish, which had Plaxton Paramount coachwork. More Leyland Olympians arrived in March but differed from the previous vehicles in having Alexander coach bodywork. They were painted in a coach livery of grey roof and between decks with blue lower panels and window surrounds. The Highland Scottish fleetname was applied in large lettering on the between decks panels. The six vehicles were divided equally between Inverness and Tain depots. The lower deck included a luggage area and consequently only 25 seats compared with the upper deck capacity of 47. These were followed by three bus seated versions. The next acquisitions were two Volvo B10M-61s with Van Hool CH49/7DT which came from Clydeside Scottish and were in Scottish Citylink livery but later received the new all-over red livery of Highland Bus and Coach. The Leyland Nationals had not proved popular and in June 1986 the fifteen buses were

At Nairn bus station D925 is working service 10 to Inverness. This Daimler Fleetline with Alexander body had come from the Fife fleet when the Ailsas returned to Kirkaldy.

Metrorider demonstrator P79 is at Farraline Park in Highland Terrier livery.

At Seafield Road depot is F374, a coach-seated Leyland Olympian with Alexander body. It is in an experimental lighter shade of grey and Highland Coaches logo.

exchanged for Leyland Leopards from the Kelvin Scottish fleet. Nine Leyland Tiger coaches joined the fleet in 1987, the first five had Duple bodies and the next four bodied by Alexander. These last four were sold to Fife Scottish in September and Highland bought from Fife five Daimler Fleetlines with Alexander bodies which were already fourteen years old. Originally new to Aberdeen Corporation (2) and Dundee Corporation (3), they were followed by another four from Strathtay Scottish which had also been new to the Aberdeen fleet in 1973.

In 1988 the vogue was for minibuses and five Renault S56s with Alexander B25F bodies were taken into stock. They were branded as Highland Terriers and carried the logo of a white West Highland terrier. In July six Leyland Leopards with Alexander bus bodies were purchased from Fife Scottish and also three Leopards with Duple Dominant coach bodies. The autumn brought more second-hand Leopards with four from Clydeside Scottish in September which had Alexander bus bodies of the type with wide entrance and panoramic windows. In November Midland Scottish supplied four more which, along with most of the Leopard intake, were used as replacements for the lightweight Fords.

In September an MCW Metrorider demonstrator was used for two weeks and in November was purchased and painted in Highland Terrier livery. The only purchases in 1989 were minibuses, two Mercedes-Benz coaches with 24 seats and three Freight Rover buses.

The last vehicles before privatisation were all second-hand. From Kelvin Scottish came seven Alexander-bodied Dodge minibuses and one Duple-bodied Leyland Tiger coach. Fife Scottish supplied four Alexander-bodied Daimler Fleetlines, originally new to Alexander Midland and five Alexander bus-bodied Leyland Leopards had been new to Eastern Scottish.

Number XS 4409, Albion PR145 with Cowieson B39F body, is passing through Fort Augustus on its way to Inverness. It was acquired with the Mcrae & Dick business in 1947 but was new to Young's Bus Services Ltd in 1947, moving to Milne of Montrose in 1942.

This Bedford OWB with Duple B28F body had been new to RS Waters, John O'Groats Mail Service and passed to Mowatt Brothers before joining the Highland fleet in 1952 and taking fleet number C24.

At Dounreay in its last year of service is E65, a Guy Arab II with Northern Counties body. New in 1947 it had platform doors fitted in 1960 and would soon be replaced by Lowlanders.

Number E72 was not popular on Inverness Town Services as the platform doors slowed boarding. It is seen on Route 4 to Culduthel, passing Station Square.

At Farraline Park is K89, a Strachan-bodied Guy Arab III, about to work a Town Service to Holm Mills. Alongside is C38, a Bedford SB with Burlingham C30F body.

At Needlefield garage following a repaint is B26, an AEC Reliance with Alexander coachwork. It had been fitted for one man operation.

Number K7, EAG 897, a Guy Arab UF 6HLW with Alexander C30CT body, was new to Western SMT in 1952 and is seen in Farraline Park. Thirty-six of these vehicles were transferred to Highland between 1963 and 1965. Seating capacities varied and those 30 seaters with a toilet had that facility removed and the seating capacity increased.

This 1970 view shows Bristol Lodekka L12 in the new double-deck livery at Farraline Park. In 1971 this vehicle returned to Scottish Omnibuses where it stayed until being withdrawn in 1975.

Nairn bus station is where CD5 awaits its return to Inverness via the villages of Croy and Cawdor. This Bedford VAS1 has a Duple Midland DP28F body. Originally numbered C26 it was changed to CD5 to denote the diesel engine. (GW)

At Thurso garage is B57, an AEC Regal III with Burlingham C35F body. It passed into the Highland fleet in 1964 from Scottish Omnibuses. (GW)

Sinclair Street, Thurso is the location of the first Albion Lowlander transferred to Highland. AL14 had been new to Central SMT in 1963 and moved north in 1965. (MC)

Former Western SMT Albion Lowlander, AL3, had bodywork by Northern Counties and is seen at Dounreay bus park in 1974 having been painted in the new livery of Peacock Blue and Poppy Red. (PTP)

This 1965 Scottish Show exhibit was CD13, a Bedford VAM had Alexander C24FM body and the mail compartment at the rear is shown in this view. It was based at Thurso and regularly worked the mail service to Bettyhill and Tongue, formerly operated by Peter Burr. (GW)

Number CD15 is seen leaving Portree Square on the Isle of Skye for Kyleakin. This Bedford VAM5 with Alexander body is in the blue and grey coach livery.

To overcome a vehicle shortage in 1967, Alexander Midland supplied three Alexander-bodied Leyland PS1 coaches. J9 is still in Midland blue at Farraline Park about to work a Town Service. (GW)

At Tain depot is Leyland PD2 with ECW body, number JD6 which had just worked the service 22 from Inverness.

In Fort William after having worked service 19 from Inverness is AV7, an Albion Viking with Alexander body. It was new to Central SMT in 1966 with a manually operated one-piece coach door. This was replaced with folding doors by Highland. (MC)

Number T12 is looking very smart in a new livery at Portree. A Ford 570E with Duple Yeoman body, it has been fitted for one man operation. It was new to Simpson of Rosehearty and passed to Alexander Northern before joining the Highland fleet in 1967.

This Guy Arab IV with Northern Counties body is at Farraline Park. E2 displays the damage to a nearside front top-deck window.

Bob Kennedy is helping one of his elderly passengers at a remote lane end. On his retirement the service passed to Highland, but the vehicle, SX 7039, a Bedford OB with Duple body, was not operated.

In Fort William bus station about to depart for Kinlochleven is BA19, an AEC Reliance with Willowbrook body from the David MacBrayne fleet.

Number T153, an Alexander-bodied Ford R1114, is outside Nairn depot. Large numbers of Fords with Duple and Alexander bodies were purchased at this time.

Six Daimler Fleetlines with Northern Counties bodies were acquired from Western SMT in August 1978. D8 is at Farraline Park.

The first new double-deckers for Highland since 1951 were ECW-bodied Leyland Fleetlines including D8 which is outside Inverness Post Office in Queensgate on a cross town route from Raigmore Hospital to St Valery Avenue.

Another Queensgate view is of Leyland National N6.

Highland acquired this Alexander 'M' type Leyland Leopard from Alexander Northern. L50 is at Farraline Park awaiting departure to Edinburgh. It was later repainted in Scottish Citylink blue and yellow livery.

The first Leyland Atlantean for Highland was this former Grampian Regional Transport example. Approaching Farraline Park, A1 is turning from Academy Street into Strothers Lane and shows how the bottom part of the central doors had been panelled over instead of being removed. (IMGS)

Ex-Newton travel Volvo with Van Hool body, V817 is getting ready to depart from Inverness for Thurso.

Alexander-bodied Leyland Leopard L804N was one which came from Kelvin Scottish in exchange for Leyland Nationals in 1986.

Number F373, one of the coach-seated Leyland Olympians allocated to Inverness depot is seen in original livery on a not untypical wet July day at Fort William. (IMGS)

At Raigmore Hospital is D920 still in Fife livery. This Alexander-bodied Daimler Fleetline had served the Midland, Northern and Fife companies before joining the Highland fleet in 1988.

HIGHLAND OMNIBUSES LTD.

COACH TOURS

FROM

INVERNESS

SEASON 1968

Coach Departure Point and Booking and Enquiry Office:—

FARRALINE PARK BUS STATION (tel. 33371/2)

AFTERNOON TOURS

11 GLEN AFFRIC   FARE 8/-

May to September — Daily.

Leave 1400 hrs. Return approx. 1845 hrs. Loch Ness, Drummadrochit, Glen Urquhart, Invercannich, Glen Affric (stop), Invercannich (Tea), Struy, Kilmorack Falls, Beauly, Inverness.

12 FOUR LOCHS AND FALLS OF FOYERS   FARE 7/-

May to September — Wednesdays and Fridays.

Leave 1400 hrs. Return approx. 1730 hrs. Dores, Falls of Foyers (stop), Foyers, arrive 1535 (Tea). Depart 1605, Pass of Inverfarigaig, Errogie, Drumashie, Inverness.

13 LOCH NESS CIRCULAR AND FORT AUGUSTUS ABBEY TOUR   FARE 8/-

May — Sundays and Thursdays.
June to September — Daily.

Leave 1415 hrs. Return approx. 1830 hrs. Dores, Pass of Inverfarigaig, Falls of Foyers (stop), White-bridge Inn, Fort Augustus, arrive 1630 (Tea). Depart 1700, Invermoriston, Glen More, Drummadrochit, Lochend, Inverness.

14 FALLS OF ROGIE AND STRATHPEFFER   FARE 7/-

May to September — Thursdays and Sundays.

Leave 1415 hrs. Return approx. 1830 hrs. Beauly, Muir of Ord, Falls of Rogie (stop), Contin, Strathpeffer, arrive 1630 (Tea). Depart 1700, Dingwall, Muir of Ord, Beauly, Inverness.

16 LOSSIEMOUTH AND ELGIN CATHEDRAL   FARE 7/-

June to September — Wednesdays and Sundays.

Leave 1400 hrs. Return approx. 1845 hrs. Nairn, Auldearn, Forres, Elgin, Lossiemouth (Tea). Return same route.

17 LOCH MORLICH, GLEN MORE LODGE AND CAIRNGORMS   FARE 9/-

May to September — Mondays, Wednesdays, Fridays and Sundays.

Leave 1400 hrs. Return approx. 1915 hrs. Daviot, Loch Moy, Tomatin, Slochd Summit, Carr Bridge, Aviemore, Coylum Bridge, Loch Morlich, Glen More (and Ski Grounds), Glen More Lodge, Coylum Bridge, Boat of Garten, Carr Bridge, Slochd, Inverness.

18 BLACK ISLE CIRCULAR   FARE 8/-

June to September — Tuesdays and Thursdays.

Leave 1415 hrs. Return approx. 1830 hrs. Beauly, Conon Bridge, Balblair, Cromarty (Tea), Rosemarkie,

SHORT TOURS

19 CULLODEN MOOR BATTLEFIELD AND INVERNESS CIRCULAR   FARE 4/6

Mid-May to September — Daily.

Leave 1030 hrs and 1500 hrs. Return approx. 1230 hrs. and 1700 hrs. Longman, Beauly Firth, Cameron Barracks, Allanfearn, Balloch, Cumberland Stone, Culloden Battlefield, Inshes, Culcabock, Kingsmills, Muirfield, Lochardil, Boar Stone, Torbreck, Holm Mills, Ness Islands, War Memorial, Castle, St Andrew's Cathedral, Tommahurich, Caledonian Canal, Leachkin, Craig Dunain, Muirtown Locks, Ness Bridge, Queen Mary's House, Steeple.

20 LOCH ASHIE   FARE 4/-

June, July and August — Mondays, Thursdays and Fridays.

Leave 1915 hrs. Return approx. 2045 hrs. Dores, Kindrummond (stop), Loch Duntelchaig, Loch Ashie, Essich, Inverness.

21 FINDHORN AND CULBIN SANDS   FARE 5/6

July and August — Sundays.

Leave 1900 hrs. Return approx. 2200 hrs. Nairn, Auldearn, Forres, Kinloss, Findhorn. Return same route.

22 FORTROSE AND ROSEMARKIE   FARE 5/6

June, July and August — Wednesdays and Sundays.

Leave 1900 hrs. Return approx. 2145 hrs. Clachnaharry, Bogroy, Beauly, Munlochy, Avoch, Fortrose, Rosemarkie. Return same route.

23 GLEN CONVINTH AND LOCH NESS   FARE 4/6

June, July and August — Tuesdays.

Leave 1900 hrs. Return approx. 2100 hrs. Clachnaharry, Beauly Firth, Bogroy, Moniack Bridge, Lovat Country, Glen Convinth, Drummadrochit, Loch Ness

Number B20, a 1959 AEC Reliance with Alexander coach body, has the older style of fleetname on the lower panel as well as the later 'Highland Omnibuses' on the waistband. It is waiting to leave Inverness on a service bus duty to Dornoch.

Four new Leyland Royal Tigers with Alexander coachwork were purchased in 1987 but were sold after three months to Fife (3) and Lowland (1). Z277 is in grey and blue coach livery and has extra large fleetnames on the side panels. It is in the depot at Seafield Road.

The bus station at Dounreay is the location of the first Ailsa to be supplied originally to W Alexander & Sons (Fife) in 1975. The front engine necessitated a separate door for the driver's cab. Ten Ailsas moved to Highland in 1980 to displace the last of the Lowlanders but returned to Fife in 1990 in exchange for some Fleetlines and Leopards. G1 is now preserved as Fife FRA1, its original number.

One of the last vehicles acquired new by Highland is Q406S. This Dodge S56 with 21 seat Alexander body is in Queensgate, Inverness on service 28 to Culloden, not the battlefield but the large housing development nearby.

by WILMOT
H. FOWKE,

Engineer and Manager, Highland
Transport Co., Ltd.

The Highland gas bus in its latest form.

OPERATING RESULTS

WITH

Effecting Substantial

Economies in P.S.V.

Working Costs

THE principles governing the operation of a suction gas plant—or as it is more commonly termed in engineering circles, producer gas—is well known, for the principle has been used—notably in steel works—for many years. The plant under review consists essentially of (1) a combustion chamber, with fuel hopper immediately above it, (2) water-cooled tuyère, (3) expansion chamber, (4) filter, and (5) hand-operated air-mixing valve. The principal difference between this plant, which is produced by Gilford (H.S.G.) Ltd., and others is the introduction of a small jet of water into the fire, giving what is known as a "wet" fire.

The chassis is a Gilford type CF.176, fitted with a 6-cylinder A.E.C. petrol engine of 8.1 litres capacity, compression being raised to 6 to 1. Owing to the lower calorific value of gas it is necessary to use an engine of considerably greater capacity than that of a petrol engine in order to obtain the same performance, but the flexibility and ability of the gas fuel engine to hold on to top gear is in marked contrast to either petrol or diesel.

In France a supercharger ("Compresseur") is frequently fitted, and this restores a lot of lost power, so that an engine, running without alteration on supercharged gas, suffers a power drop of less than 10 per cent. compared with the same engine on petrol (non-supercharged). I recently had the opportunity of observing tests made in France with various vehicles ranging from the private car up to a heavy Latil, with trailer, of 23 tons gross weight, and the use of the supercharger gives a very marked improvement in power.

The Highland Transport Co.'s vehicle could, if the body were seated to the minimum clearances, seat 36 passengers, but as 32 is the company's standard capacity the 31 seats actually fitted entails a loss of one seat only. The plant is housed in a completely isolated compartment at the off-side rear end, the opposite side being a luggage compartment or, in the event of a specially long journey away from home, a space for reserve fuel.

In regular service, however, up to 200 miles are being run on one filling of anthracite, or 160 miles on "Suncole" — a low-temperature coke. Each of these fuels possesses distinctive characteristics, and it has not yet been decided which is the better. It is essential to use only the very best grade in both cases and to maintain the plant scrupulously clean. The weight of the plant adds

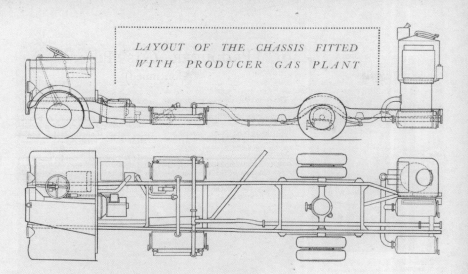

LAYOUT OF THE CHASSIS FITTED
WITH PRODUCER GAS PLANT

PRODUCER GAS

approximately 6 cwt. to the tare of the corresponding petrol vehicle, the one in question being 6 tons 1 cwt.

The body was built and fitted in the company's workshops in Inverness, during which time frequent consultations were held with the

Ministry of Transport representatives, with the result that when the vehicle was presented for inspection by the certifying officer, including the tilt test, alterations of only minor character were required.

The vehicle entered regular service on January 2 this year, and, in-

cluding its testing period, has at the time of writing run some 7,000 miles, the consumption averaging 2 lb. to 2.2 lb. per mile, and fuel cost 0.65d. to 0.7d. per mile. Compare this with 1.8d. for petrol and 1.0d. for diesel oil! This vehicle's schedule at present is 1,200 miles a week; it

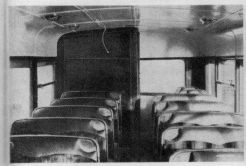

Looking towards the rear of the vehicle, the neat cabinet housing the producer gas plant is seen.

With the rear inspection doors open, a good view of the lower portion of the equipment is obtained.

PRODUCER GAS PLANT
(Continued)

Underneath the driver's seat are the fan and two-way valve.

The question of gas propulsion was first considered in the summer of 1936, after an inspection and test of the Gilford demonstration truck which had been sent through to Edinburgh and Glasgow, principally through the indefatigable efforts of the Duke of Montrose. After much planning it was unanimously decided by the directors of this company to give the system a thorough trial, and accordingly the present chassis was obtained and the vehicle completed

country annually for imported oil with its adverse effect on the national trade balance. A petrol vehicle doing 8 m.p.g. and a diesel at 14 m.p.g. is approximately equivalent to a producer-gas engine vehicle consuming 2 lb. of solid fuel per mile, and it can be accepted that lighter or heavier vehicles vary in the above proportion, and the fillip given to our coal industry by the extended use of the gas vehicle can readily be visualised.

This near-side view of the engine shows the screw-down valve for operating on gas.

works out of Inverness each day, where all re-fuelling, cleaning (and the usual maintenance) are carefully attended to. Filters are opened up and thoroughly cleaned once a week, and de-clinkered and refuelled daily, the fire-box and hopper being emptied every second day, the unburnt fuel so removed being screened and put back into the hopper.

It is anticipated that engine lubricant will yield greater mileage owing to a true gas mixture being used as compared with the saturated mixtures delivered into both petrol and diesel cylinders, with a corresponding reduction of cylinder and piston wear, but this, of course, has yet to be proved.

Need for Low Costs

The sparse population of the North of Scotland is probably well known, but how many people are aware, for instance, that the density of population for each of the counties of Inverness and Ross and Cromarty is only 18 persons per square mile, for Sutherlandshire 9, and Caithness 35? It is not surprising, therefore, that receipts per mile are of a low order; while, on the other side, supplies cost more. So also does maintenance, owing largely to road conditions, which are inferior to those in most counties farther south, and consequently any means which seem to offer a reasonable chance of reducing operating costs have simply got to be considered.

in Inverness. Incidentally, it was the first entirely new body built in the Highland Company's shops.

True the great appeal is that of economical working, but issues of a far larger order are involved ; if this country is again unfortunately involved in a major conflict, it is a practical certainty that little or no petrol or oil will be available for private cars, and that both passenger and goods services will, perforce, be drastically curtailed. One has not forgotten the petrol rationing of 1914-18, and to-day the consumption by the services is infinitely greater.

In normal times, however, a vast sum of money is sent out of the

In most European countries, and particularly in France, Germany and Italy, immense progress has already been made in the use of this type of fuel, and it is within my personal knowledge that in the first two named countries operators are encouraged to use this type of vehicle by the direct incentive of very substantial rebates on vehicle taxation. How long can this country afford to ignore the obvious all-round advantages accruing to the adoption of this system ?

As my concluding remark I cannot do better than refer readers to an article entitled "For a National Emergency," which appeared in The Autocar of January 28.

OFFICES, DEPOTS & OUTSTATIONS

Head Office. Station Square, Inverness January 1952 to 1958
Farraline Park, Inverness 1958 to 19th July 1972
Seafield Road, Inverness 20th July 1958 onwards
Central Works, Needlefield, Longman Road, Inverness until October 1975.
Seafield Road, Inverness from October 1975. (formerly Highland Transport Company Limited premises)

Aviemore	Myrtlefield Road	Depot	
Dingwall	Railway station	Office	Closed
Dingwall	South Road	Depot	Closed
Cromarty		Outstation	Closed
Diabeg		Outstation	Closed
Garve		Outstation	Closed
Laide		Outstation	Closed
Fortrose		Depot	Closed
Dornoch	Drill Hall	Office	
Dornoch	Station Road	Depot (now sub-depot)	
Helmsdale		Outstation	
Lairg		Outstation	
Fort William	Inverlochy Road	Depot	
Fort William		Bus Station	Opened 1975
Grantown on Spey		Depot	Closed
Inverness	Carse Road	Depot	Closed
Inverness	Farraline Park	Office	
Inverness	Longman Road	Depot	Closed
Inverness	Seafield Road	Depot	
Kinlochleven		Depot	
Nairn	High Street	Office	
Nairn	Riverside	Depot	Closed
Nairn	King Street	Depot & Bus Station	
Oban	Soroba Lane	Depot	Transferred
Tain	Scotburn Road	Depot	
Fearn		Outstation	
Portmahomack		Outstation	
Thurso	Janet Street	Depot & Office	
Bettyhill		Outstation	
Mey		Outstation	
Wick	Back Bridge Street	Office	
Wick	Station Road	Depot	
Dunbeath		Outstation	
Lybster		Outstation	
John O'Groats		Outstation	
Isle of Harris	Tarbert	Depot	Transferred
Isle of Islay	Port Ellen	Depot	Closed
Isle of Mull	Tobermory	Depot	Closed
Isle of Skye	Ardvasar	Depot	Closed
Isle of Skye	Park Road, Portree	Depot	Transferred

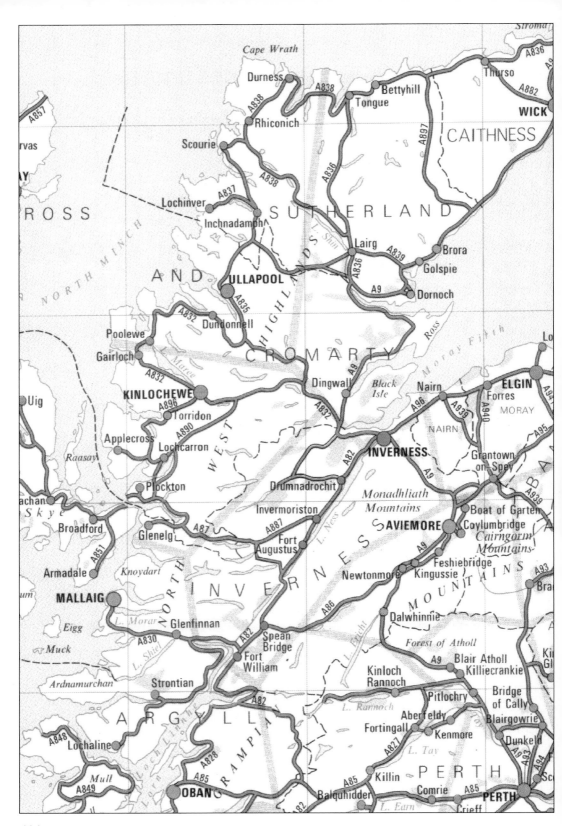

The transfer of most of the MacBraynes mainland operation to Highland in 1970 included the route from Oban to Fort William. UGB 428 is at Kinlochleven, and although it has yet to be repainted into Highland Livery, it is displaying B43, its Highland fleet number.

Former Ribble Leyland Royal Tiger with Leyland body, J3 shows how the rear end was rebuilt to accommodate the carrying of skis. This view was taken at Kincraig which is a few miles south of Aviemore.

Depot allocation plates were carried for part of the 1950s and 1960s. These were cast metal with the code letter in base metal against a painted background.

Codes were:
C   Caithness (Wick or Thurso)
D   Dingwall
DR   Dornoch
I   Inverness

Codes were re-introduced in late 1975 with yellow plates and black lettering being changed later to either silver on red or blue on grey depending on the vehicle livery.

A   Aviemore
DH   Dornoch
DL   Dingwall
F   Fort William
I   Inverness

N   Nairn
O   Oban
P   Portree
T   Thurso
TN   Tain
TY   Tobermory
W   Wick

From 8th September 1985 codes were again changed to become a suffix to the fleet number wherever it appeared.

A   Aviemore
F   Fort William
N   Nairn
R   Ross-shire
S   Inverness
T   Thurso
V   Reserve fleet
W   Wick

LIVERIES

These descriptions are very much a generalisation as liveries were adapted to suit the individual lines of many of the vehicles. The dates shown do not indicate that the whole fleet was repainted but that a new livery was adopted for a style of bodywork new to the fleet.

Highland Transport Company Limited.

1931:
Double-deck buses:
Roof - White with Crimson Lake rainwater gutters
Upper deck window surrounds - White
Band below upper deck windows - White with Crimson Lake beadings
Upper deck panels - Crimson Lake with Gold linings top and bottom
Lower deck window frames and surrounds - White
Band below lower deck windows - White with Crimson Lake beadings
Lower deck panels - Crimson Lake with Gold linings top and bottom and around wings
Wings and wheels - Crimson Lake
Fleetname - HIGHLAND in Gold on lower deck panels

1933:
Single-deck buses:
Roof, window frames and surrounds - White
Panels, wings and wheels - Crimson Lake
Waist moulding line - White
Fleetname - HIGHLAND in Gold on panels

By **1936** some vehicles carried the Golden Eagle motif on the panels

1939-45:
Repaints were in all-over Grey.

1946-51:
Double-deck buses:
Roof, upper deck window frames and surrounds - Crimson Lake
Band below upper deck windows - Cream
Upper deck panels, lower deck window frames and surrounds - Crimson Lake
Band below lower deck windows - Cream
Lower deck panels, wings, wheels and bonnet - Crimson Lake
Fleetname - HIGHLAND in Crimson Lake on band below lower deck windows
Fleet number - Cream
Golden Eagle on side panels

Single-deck buses:
All crimson Lake except for metal window louvres and waistband in Cream
Golden Eagle on side panels

Highland Omnibuses Limited

1952:
Double-deck buses:
Roof, upper deck window frames and surrounds - Crimson Lake
Band below upper deck windows - Cream
Upper deck panels - Crimson Lake
Between decks band - Cream
Lower deck window frames and surrounds - Cream
Band below lower deck windows - Cream
Lower deck panels, wheels and bonnet - Crimson Lake
Wings - Black
Fleetname - HIGHLAND in Gold, located centrally above or below lower deck windows
Fleet number - Gold, or on cast metal plates with painted background

Single-deck buses
Roof - Crimson Lake
Band on cove panels - Cream

Window frames and surrounds - Crimson Lake
Band below windows - Cream
Panels and bonnet - Crimson Lake
Wings - Cream
Wheels - Crimson Lake
Fleetname - HIGHLAND in Gold on panels
Fleet number - Gold

1953:
Coaches (Duple Vista)
Roof - Crimson Lake
Window frames, surrounds, panels and bonnet - Cream
Waistband, flashes, wings and wheels - Crimson Lake
Fleetname - HIGHLAND in Crimson Lake on panels

Coaches (Burlingham Seagull)
Roof - Cream
Window surrounds - Crimson Lake
Panels above curved mouldings - Cream
Panels below curved mouldings - Crimson Lake
Wheels - Crimson Lake and Cream
Fleetname - HIGHLAND in Gold on Crimson Lake panels

1956:
Coaches
Roof - Cream
Window surrounds - Crimson Lake
Panels and wheels - Cream
Fleetname - HIGHLAND in Crimson Lake on Cream panels

1961:
Coaches
Roof - Cream
Window surrounds - Crimson Lake
Waistband and wheels - Cream
Panels - Crimson Lake
Fleetname - Highland Omnibuses in Gold script on waistband

1965:
Golden Eagle motif added to the panels

1964-68:
Single-deck buses and dual-purpose vehicles
Roof and waistband - Cream
Window frames and surrounds, panels and wheels - Crimson Lake
Fleetname - Highland in Gold script on panels

1967:
Double-deck buses
Roof - Red
Upper deck window frames and surrounds - Cream
Upper deck panels - Red
Lower deck window frames and surrounds - Cream

Lower deck panels - Red
Wings - Black
Wheels - Cream
Fleetname - HIGHLAND in Gold above lower deck windows
Fleet number - Gold

1967:
Coaches
Grey and Blue livery adopted applied in ways to suit body styling
Golden Eagle motif and fleetname Highland Omnibuses in Gold script

1968-70:
Single-deck buses
Roof - Red
Window frames, surrounds and panels - Red
Waistband and skirt - Cream
Fleetname - Highland in Gold script on waistband

1970:
Double-deck buses
Roof and upper deck window surrounds - Peacock Blue
Upper deck panels - Poppy Red
Lower deck window frames and surrounds - Peacock Blue
Lower deck panels - Poppy Red
Wings - Black
Wheels - Grey
Fleetname - HIGHLAND in Gold letters above lower deck windows (From 1976, White on lower deck panels)
Golden Eagle motif on lower deck panels (later moved to upper deck panels)
Fleet number - Gold (White from 1976)

1970:
Single-deck buses
Roof, window frames and surrounds - Peacock Blue
Panels - Poppy Red
Wheels - Grey
Golden Eagle motif and fleetname Highland Omnibuses in Gold script
Fleet number - Gold (later White)

1973:
Coaches
Roof - Grey
Window frames, surrounds and waistband - Blue
Panels - Grey
Skirt - Blue
Wheels - Grey
Fleetname - Highland Omnibuses in Gold script on waistband
Golden Eagle motif on panels

1976:
Coaches
Roof - Blue
Panels - Grey
Windscreen surround and skirt - Blue
Fleetname - Highland in White (later in Blue and changing to Highland Scottish)
Fleet number - White

1979:
Double-deck buses
Roof - Peacock Blue
Upper deck window frames, surround and panels - Poppy Red
Between decks band - Grey
Lower deck window frames, surround and panels - Poppy Red
Wheels - Grey
Fleetname - Highland Scottish in Blue on Grey band, Highland in White below windscreen
Fleet number - White
Golden Eagle motif on upper deck panels

1980:
Single-deck buses
Leyland Nationals
Roof, window frames and surrounds - Poppy Red
Panels - Grey
Skirt - Poppy Red
Fleetname - Highland SCOTTISH in Blue on Grey panels
Others
All main areas - Poppy Red
Waistband - Grey
Fleetname - Highland SCOTTISH in Blue on Grey above front wheels

1980:
Double-deck buses
All main areas - Poppy Red
Band below upper deck windows - Grey
Band between decks - Grey
Fleetname - Highland SCOTTISH in Blue on Grey between decks band

1988:
Double-deck buses
Roof, window surrounds and skirt - Ayres Red
Panels between lower deck windows and skirt - Grey
Fleetname - HIGHLAND SCOTTISH in Blue on Grey panels
Fleet number - White

1988:
single-deck buses
Roof, waistband and skirt - Ayres Red
Panels between windows and skirt - Grey
Fleetname - HIGHLAND SCOTTISH in Blue on Grey panels
Fleet number - White

1991:
All Double-deck buses
All over Ayres Red with Grey band above lower deck windows
Fleetname - HIGHLAND BUS AND COACH in Red on Grey band
Wheels - Black
Fleet number - White

1991:
All single-deck buses
All over Ayres Red with Grey waistband
Fleetname - Highland Bus and Coach in Red on Grey band
Wheels - Black
Fleet number - White

Coaches
All over Ayres Red
Fleetname - Highland Bus and Coach in Yellow
Wheels - Black
Fleet number - White

This Strachan bodied Karrier had served several owners before entering the Highland fleet in 1968. D1 is at Diabeg in Wester Ross.

Kennex-bodied Austin J4, MB5 is at Needlefield garage having been acquired from S McGregor of Dornoch.

The large flap beneath the number plate is the connecting point for the heating duct on the Alexander-bodied Albion Lowlander, AL26. (AJD)

Number BA11 is one of sixteen AEC Reliances with Alexander coach bodies transferred from Scottish Omnibuses in 1969. These were the first 36ft long vehicles in the Highland fleet. It is parked at Riverside, Thurso. (MC)

BCS 252C. Originally hired from Western SMT to cover late deliveries of new buses, this Albion Lowlander LR1 with Northern Counties body was eventually purchased and took fleetnumber AL49. (AJD)

YMS 702R. Hired from Strathtay in 1988 was this Ailsa B55-10 with Alexander body.

WSD 756K (H12) was converted by Western SMT into a breakdown truck from Leyland Leopard L2366.

MSD 367. This Leyland PD3 with Northern Counties lowbridge body from Western SMT is leaving Farraline Park during its stay with Highland in 1975. (AJD)

By bus to Bavaria

Drivers Brem Macleod and Jock Watt, of Highland Omnibuses, went from Inverness to Augsburg, Bavaria, in November—and took a nine-year-old Albion double-decker with them.

But then neither Brem nor his co-driver are strangers to driving Highland buses on the Continent since both have taken hires and tours abroad on several previous occasions.

The latest trip, to boost Inverness and the Highlands, was, according to Brem, an uneventful, trouble-free drive there and back, over 1000 miles each way.

'The only thing broken was a window, and it was replaced while we were in Bavaria,' he said.

The Albion Lowlander, originally in the Western SMT fleet, was welcomed by a silver band reception and a large crowd on arrival in Augsburg, a 'twin' town with Inverness.

Not unnaturally, a double-decker in Highland's blue/red livery took a trick with the locals during the four days it was parked in the town square.

The bus had been converted to house an exhibition for the trip organised by Inverness Junior Chamber of Commerce to give Augsburg on-the-spot impressions of the Scottish Highlands.

Seats were removed from the lower deck to provide space for an exhibition and the top deck was adapted to become a mini cinema.

10. JANUARY 1974

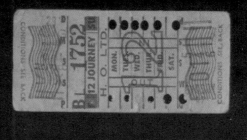

114

FLEETLIST

Year Rec'd	Fleet No.	Reg.No	Chassis	Body	Seating	Withdrawn	Former operator	Year New
1930	1	ST 3290	Vulcan VWD	?	CH26	1930	Inverness & District	1925
1930	27	ST 3964	AEC 411	?	B30R	1932	Inverness & District	1926
1930	28	ST 3946	Albion PK26	?	B29R	1943	Inverness & District	1926
1930	29	ST4066	Albion PF26	?	CH18	1934	Inverness & District	1926
1930	30	ST 4324	Albion PM28	?	B32	1947	Inverness & District	1927
1930	31	ST 4721	Albion PM28	?	B32	1943	Inverness & District	1927
1930	32	ST 4983	Albion PM28	?	B32	1950	Inverness & District	1928
1930	33	ST 5094	Albion PNA26	?	C26	?	Inverness & District	1928
1930	34	ST 5313	Albion PM28	?	B32	?	Inverness & District	1928
1930	35	ST 5451	Ford A	?	20	1946	Inverness & District	1929
1930	36	ST 5386	AEC 426	Hall Lewis	B32	1939	Inverness & District	1928
1930	37	ST 5675	Ford A	?	20	1946	Inverness & District	1929
1930	38	ST 5583	Albion PJ26	?	B26	1946	Inverness & District	1928
1930	39	ST 5645	Albion PJ26	?	B26	1937	Inverness & District	1929
1930	40	ST 5674	Albion PJ26	?	B26	?	Inverness & District	1929
1930	41	ST 5751	Albion PJ26	?	B26	1947	Inverness & District	1928
1930	42	JS 2795	Albion PJ26	?	B26	1935	Inverness & District	1926
1930	43	JS 3068	Albion PK26	?	B26	1944	Inverness & District	1927
1930	44-45	ST 6119/20	Albion PM28	?	B32	1951		
1930	46	ST 6102	Albion PKA26	?	B26	1950		
1930	47	ST 6103	Albion PKA26	?	C26F	1946		
1930	48	ST 6176	Albion PMA 28	?	B32R	1951		
1930	49	ST 6198	Albion PMA 28	?	B32R	1947		
1930	50	ST 6234	AEC Regal	Porteous	C26	1946		
1930	51-52	ST 6145/6	AECRegal	Porteous	B32R	1946		
1930	?	ST 6301	Morris	?	14	1935		
1930	1	TU 9244	Ford A	?	B14	1931	Portree Motor Coach	1928
1930	2	ST 6023	Ford A	?	B14	1935	Portree Motor Coach	1930
1930	3	ST 4580	Dodge	?	B14	1933	Portree Motor Coach	1927
1930	4	JS 3064	Morris	?	B14	1932	Portree Motor Coach	1927
1930	5	ST 5105	Austin	Car	4	1935	Portree Motor Coach	1928
1930	6	PF 1655	Austin	Car	7	1935	Portree Motor Coach	1926
1930	7	GB 5276	Humber 15.9 hp	Car	4	1931	Portree Motor Coach	1924
1930	8	GD 8767	Armstrong Siddley	Car	4	1931	Portree Motor Coach	1927
1930	9	ST 4260	Austin	Car	4	1932	Portree Motor Coach	1926
1930	10	RS 5386	Sunbeam	Car	4	1932	Portree Motor Coach	1924
1930	11	ST 5463	Ford A	Car	4	1932	Portree Motor Coach	1929
1930	12	ST 3057	Wolsley	Car	4	1932	Portree Motor Coach	1924
1931	8	ST 6644	Albion PMA 28	?	B32F	1946		
1931	7	HX 1388	AEC Regent	Strachan	H26/24R	1942	AEC Demonstrator	1930
1932	9/10	ST 6982/3	Albion PW65	?	B32F	1952/?		
1932		ST 6990	Albion Sp LBA41	Weymann	C20F	1935		
1932		ST 7025	Bedford	?	?	1935		
1932		ST 7113	Albion Sp LBA41	Weymann	C20F	1935		
1932	11	SK 1425	Chevrolet LO	Briggs	14	1933	Robertson, Wick	1928
1932	12	SK 1491	Chevrolet	Briggs	14	1933	Robertson, Wick	1928
1932	14	SK 1502	Chevrolet LP	Briggs	14	1934	Robertson, Wick	1928
1932	15	SK 1561	Chevrolet LQ	Briggs	14	1934	Robertson, Wick	1929
1932	16	SK 1658	AJS Pilot	?	20	1935	Robertson, Wick	1930
1932	26	SK 1763	Albion PKA26	?	B20FM	1940	Robertson, Wick	1931
1933	55	ST 7195	AEC Regal	Park Royal	B32R	1954		
1933	11	ST 7347	Ford	?	C14	1935		
1933	53	SK 1507	Albion PK26	Spicer	26	1950	Hunter, Castletown	1928
1933	18	SK 1689	Chevrolet U	?	20	1933	Johnstone, Castletown	1930
1933	22	SE 3363	Reo	?	?	1944	Wares, Castletown	1930
1933		SK 1820	Reo	?	?	?	Wares, Castletown	1932
1933	25	SK 1657	BAT	?	B20	1935	Begg, Wick	1933
1933	57	RG 2821	Albion PH49	?	B20	1947	D Allan, Watten	1932
1933	19	GE 3823	Reo Sprinter	?	?	1944	?	1929
1933	54	MV 1878	AEC Regal	?	32	1954	AEC Demonstrator	1932

Year Rec'd	Fleet No.	Reg.No	Chassis	Body	Seating	Withdrawn	Former operator	Year New
1933	56	US 1960	Albion PW65	?	B32	?	Albion Demonstrator	1933
1934	58	ST 7752	Ford	Porteous	C14	1947		
1934	59-61	ST 7762-4	Albion PW67	Cowieson	B32R	1955/6		
1935	62	ST 8029	Albion PW67	Cowieson	B32R	1956		
1935	65	ST 8043	Albion LBA41	?	B14	1947		
1935	63	CP 6760	Albion PM28	Massey	B32	1948	Hebble	1928
1936	67	ST 8651	Bedford WTL	?	C?F	1948		
1936	68/9	ST 8652/3	Albion PW141	Cowieson	B32R	1952/4		
1937	72	ST 9081	Rolls Royce	Limousine	7	1951	Rebuilt in 1937	1926
1937	73	ST 9132	Albion PW141	Cowieson	B32R	1957		
1937	74	ST 9092	Albion PW69	Cowieson	B32R	1957		
1937	75	ST 9465	Gilford HSG/CP1	Cowieson	B31R	1951		
1937	77	ST 6461	Chevrolet	?	B14	1942	Fraser, Kiltarlity	1931
1937	78	ST 6361	Reo	?	B20	1951	Fraser, Kiltarlity	1930
1938	79	ST 9767	Albion PR145	Cowieson	B40R	1957		
1938	80	ST 9612	Albion PW141	Cowieson	B32R	1955		
1938	81	ST 9978	Albion SpCX9	Cowieson	B32R	1955		
1938	82	AST 100	Albion CX9	Cowieson	B38R	1952		
1938	84	ST 7318	AEC Regal IV	Park Royal	B32R	1951	Fraser, Lentran	1933
1938	85	ST 7851	AEC Regal IV	Walker	B32R	1953	Fraser, Lentran	1934
1938	86	ST 8167	Albion PK115	Cadogan	B30R	1949	Fraser, Lentran	1935
1938	87	ST 5535	Reo	Mitchell	B26F	1951	Fraser, Lentran	1929
1938	88	ST 6610	Reo	Emcol	B26F	1951	Fraser, Lentran	1931
1939	90	AST 318	Bedford WTB	?	?	1948		
1939	91	AST 505	Albion SpCK13	Cowieson	B35F	1957		
1940	95	SK 2433	Fordson BB	?	?	1940	Wilson, Thurso	1938
1940	96	FS 6540	Albion PH49	Cowieson	B20F	1951	SMT Edinburgh	1933
1940	94	CK 4593	Leyland TS2	Weymann	B32R	1944	Wemyss, Ardersier	1931
1940	97	SN 5643	Albion PV70	Cowieson	C32	1951	Central SMT	1932
1940	98	VD 4455	Leyland TS7T	Leyland	B38R	1955	Central SMT	1935
1941	99	WG 591	Albion PW65	Alexander	B36F	1951	W Alexander	1932
1942	100	AST 734	Albion CX9	Duple	B39F	1954		
1942	1	AST 749	TSM H5LA4	Willowbrook	B26F	1956		
1942	2	AST 806	Leyland TS11	Willowbrook	B36F	1957		
1942	5-7	AST 829-31	Bedford OWB	SMT	B32F	1960-2		
1943	12	AST 843	Bedford OWB	SMT	B32F	1959		
1943	13	AST 866	Bedford OWB	SMT	B32F	1952		
1943	14	AST 890	Bedford OWB	SMT	B32F	1960		
1944	15-8	AST 949-52	Bedford OWB	Duple	B32F	1961-4		
1944	19/20	AST 957/8	Guy Arab II	NCME	L27/28R	1963/4		
1945	22/3	BST 24/5	Bedford OWB	Duple	B32F	1956-62		
1945	24/5	BST 68/9	Guy Arab II	Weymann	L27/26R	1963		
1945	28/9	BST 91/2	Guy Arab II	Roe	L27/28R	1963		
1945	26	WG 1401	Albion PW65	MCCW	B36F	1945	W Alexander	1933
1945	27	WG 1403	Albion PW65	MCCW	B36F	1952	W Alexander	1933
1946	35/6	BST 277/8	Guy Arab II	Strachan	L27/28R	1964		
1946	37/8	BST 325/6	Guy Arab II	Strachan	L27/28R	1965-7		
1946	47	BST 570	Guy Arab II	NCME	L27/26R	1966		
1946	50	BST 573	Guy Arab II	NCME	L27/26R	1965		
1946	51/2	BST 571/2	Guy Arab II	NCME	L27/26R	1965-6		
1946	8	SK 2862	Bedford OWB	Duple	C32F	1960	Wilson, Thurso	1944
1947	41-3	BST 669-71	Guy Arab III	Strachan	B34F	1962		
1947	57/8	BST 917/8	Guy Arab III	Guy	B34R	1962		
1947	64/5	CST 270/1	Guy Arab III	NCME	L27/26R	1967		
1948	63/66	CST 272/3	Guy Arab III	NCME	L27/26R	1965		
1948	67/71	CST 697/8	Guy Arab III	Strachan	B34F	1963		
1949	83/86	DST 283/4	Guy Arab III	Strachan	B34F	1963		
1950	32/46/70	DST 928/30	Guy Arab III	Strachan	B34F	1963-5		
1951	72	EST 392	Guy Arab III	Strachan	FL31/26RD	1970		
1951	89/90/92	EST 393-5	Guy Arab III	Strachan	B34F	1968/9		
1952	H127	ATC 269	Leyland TS7	Macrae & Dick	B35R	1953	Macrae & Dick	1935
1952	Ap101/2	ST 8667/8	Albion PH115	Albion	B26F	1953/5	Macrae & Dick	1936

Year Rec'd	Fleet No.	Reg.No	Chassis	Body	Seating	Withdrawn	Former operator	Year New
1952	Ap103/4	ST 9100/1	Albion PK115	Albion	B26F	1954/5	Macrae & Dick	1937
1952	Ap105	ST 9200	Albion PK115	Albion	C26F	1957	Macrae & Dick	1937
1952	Ap106	WG 4922	Albion PW141	Walker	B32F	1957	Macrae & Dick	1936
1952	Ap107	AV 7256	Albion PW69	Walker	B34F	1956	Macrae & Dick	1935
1952	Ap108	CS 3895	Albion PH115	Stewart	B28F	1953	Macrae & Dick	1936
1952	Ap109	ST 9731	Albion PK115	Albion	B32F	1952	Macrae & Dick	1938
1952	A110	XS 4409	Albion PR145	Cowieson	B39F	1955	Macrae & Dick	1937
1952	A111/2	CST 649/50	Albion CX9	Brockhouse	B35F	1959	Macrae & Dick	1948
1952	Ap113/4	CST 890/1	Albion SpFT3l	Croft	C24F	1956/7	Macrae & Dick	1949
1952	D115/6	CST 535/635	Austin CXB	Walker	C26F	1957	Macrae & Dick	1948
1952	D117/8	DST 305/65	Austin K4LV	Churchill	C30F	1957	Macrae & Dick	1949
1952	D119	EST 560	Austin CXD	Churchill	C30F	1962	Macrae & Dick	1951
1952	D120	EST 564	Austin CXD	Kenex	C32F	1961	Macrae & Dick	1951
1952	C121	AST 893	Bedford OWB	SMT	B28F	1954	Macrae & Dick	1943
1952	C122/3	AST 933/4	Bedford OWB	Duple	B28F	1963/4	Macrae & Dick	1943
1952	C124	CST 511	Bedford OB	Croft	B26F	1957	Macrae & Dick	1948
1952	C125	FDK 570	Bedford OB	Duple	C27F	1961	Macrae & Dick	1947
1952	L126	CST 903	Commer Commando	Croft	B29F	1960	Macrae & Dick	1949
1952	J150	WG 3481	Leyland TS7	Alexander (1943)	L27/26R	1960	W Alexander	1935
1952	J151	AFG 679	Leyland TS7	Alexander (1943)	L27/26R	1960	W Alexander	1935
1952	J152	WG 3443	Leyland TS7	Alexander (1943)	L27/26R	1954	W Alexander	1935
1952	J153	WG 3486	Leyland TS7	Alexander (1943)	L27/26R	1960	W Alexander	1935
1952	J154	SN 7136	Leyland TS7	Alexander (1943)	L27/26R	1960	W Alexander	1936
1952	J155	AFG 664	Leyland TS7	Alexander (1943)	L27/26R	1960	W Alexander	1935
1952	J156	WG 3483	Leyland TS7	Alexander (1943)	L27/26R	1960	W Alexander	1935
1952	J157	WG 3511	Leyland TS7	Alexander (1943)	L27/26R	1960	W Alexander	1936
1952	J158	WG 3261	Leyland TS	Alexander (1943)	L27/26R	1959	W Alexander	1936
1952	J159	WG 3505	Leyland TS	Alexander (1943)	L27/26R	1955	W Alexander	1936
1952	J160	WG 3501	Leyland TS	Alexander (1944)	L27/26R	1959	W Alexander	1936
1952	J161	JY 5025	Leyland TS	Alexander (1945)	L27/26R	1960	W Alexander	1935
1952	J162	WE 8776	Leyland TD	Croft (1944)	L27/24R	1953	W Alexander	1930
1952	J163	CK 4878	Leyland TD	English Electric	L26/26R	1957	W Alexander	1934
1952	J164	CRA 258	Leyland TD	MCCW	L26/26R	1958	W Alexander	1937
1952	J165	CK 4627	Leyland TD	Leyland	L24/24R	1957	W Alexander	1932
1952	J166	CK 4873	Leyland TD	English Electric	L26/26R	1956	W Alexander	1934
1952	J167	ERA 80	Leyland TD5	Leyland	L26/26R	1958	W Alexander	1937
1952	J168	CRA 257	Leyland TD4	MCCW	L27/26R	1958	W Alexander	1937
1952	J169	CST 256	Leyland PD1A	Leyland	L27/26R	1965	W Alexander	1948
1952	H170/1	WG 1122/5	Leyland TS4	Alexander	B32F	1953	W Alexander	1932
1952	C172	WG 4435	Bedford WTB	Duple	C20F	1957	W Alexander	1936
1952	C173	BWG 247	Bedford OB	SMT	C25F	1962	W Alexander	1948
1952	E89	HGC 154	Guy Arab II	Weymann	H30/56R	1954	Scottish Omnibuses	1945
1952	D121	JSF 409	Austin CXD	Kenex	C32F	1961	Scottish Omnibuses	1952
1952	E87	GXE 556	Guy Arab II	Park Royal	H30/56R	1954	London Transport	1944
1952	E88	GYL 343	Guy Arab II	Park Royal	H30/56R	1954	London Transport	1945
1952	K75-80	JWS 122-7	Guy Arab II rebuilt	SOL (1952)	B39F			1963-5
1952	C24	SK 2840	Bedford OWB	Duple	B28F	1959	Mowatt Brothers	1944
1953	K81-5	JWS 128-31	Guy Arab II rebuilt	SOL (1952)	B39F			1963-5
1953	K93/87	KSC 918-9	Guy Arab II rebuilt	SOL (1953)	B39F			1963-5
1953	L2-4	CMS 291/7-8	Commer Commando	Scottish Aviation	C29F	1960/1	W Alexander	
1953	L5	CMS 289	Commer Commando	Scottish Aviation	C29F	1960/1	W Alexander	
1953	L6/7	CMS 299-300	Commer Commando	Scottish Aviation	C29F	1960/1	W Alexander	
1953	H3/4	VD 8768/9	Leyland TS8	Alexander	B32R	1957	Central SMT	1938
1953	K95-100	LSC 96-101	Guy Arab II rebuilt	SOL(1953)	C35F			1966
1955	A1	NSG 869	Albion MR9	SOL	B32F	1956		
1955	H5-8	VD 7370-73	Leyland TS7	Leyland	B32R	1958/9	Central SMT	1937
1955	E11/14	DWS 845/922	Guy Arab II	Roe	L27/26R	1963	Scottish Omnibuses	1944
1955	E16	DWS 352	Guy Arab II	NCME	L27/26R	1963	Scottish Omnibuses	1943
1956	A1-6	KST 50-5	Albion MR9	Alexander	C29F	1965/7		
1956	L8/9	CMS 2/4	Commer Commando	Scottish Aviation	C29F	1960	W Alexander	1949
1956	L10-12	CMS 9-11	Commer Commando	Scottish Aviation	C29F	1960	David Lawson	1949
1956	E9	WG 9520	Guy Arab I	Duple	L27/26R	1957	David Lawson	1942

Year Rec'd	Fleet No.	Reg.No	Chassis	Body	Seating	Withdrawn	Former operator	Year New
1956	E10	WG 9884	Guy Arab I	NCME	L27/26R	1959	David Lawson	1943
1956	E12/3	WG 9821/9921	Guy Arab I	Strachan	L27/26R	1958/62	David Lawson	1943
1956	E17/8	WG 9972/7	Guy Arab II	Roe	L27/26R	1963/59	David Lawson	1943
1956	E21/2	AMS 43/9	Guy Arab II	Roe	L27/26R	1959	David Lawson	1943/4
1956	E23/26	WG 9971/4	Guy Arab II	Roe	L27/26R	1958/9	David Lawson	1943
1956	E15	EFS 355	Guy Arab II	Weymann	L27/26R	1962	Scottish Omnibuses	1945
1956	C19-20	FFS 878/9	Bedford OB	SMT	C24F	1962	Scottish Omnibuses	1948
1956	C21	FFS 885	Bedford OB	SMT	C24F	1961	Scottish Omnibuses	1948
1956	C23/5	FFS 877/80	Bedford OB	SMT	C24F	1961/2	Scottish Omnibuses	1948
1957	B1-6	KST 651-6	AEC Monocoach	Alexander	DP41F	1966-73		
1957	B7-12	LST 501-6	AEC Reliance	Park Royal	DP41F	1973		
1957	E6	WG 9820	Guy Arab I	Strachan	L27/26R	1961	David Lawson	1943
1957	E7	WG 9976	Guy Arab I	Roe	L27/26R	1958	David Lawson	1943
1957	E8	WG 9542	Guy Arab I	Duple	L27/26R	1958	David Lawson	1942
1957	E27	WG 9922	Guy Arab I	Strachan	L27/26R	1958	David Lawson	1943
1957	E5/9	ASD 406/8	Guy Arab II	NCME	L27/26R	1961/3	Western SMT	1943
1957	E30/31	GYL 413/421	Guy Arab II	NCME	L27/26R	1963	Western SMT	1945
1957	E1-3	EFS 351/50/52	Guy Arab II	Weymann	L27/26R	1965/6	Scottish Omnibuses	1945
1957	E4	DWS 921	Guy Arab II	Roe	L27/26R	1965	Scottish Omnibuses	1944
1957	C26	FFS 887	Bedford OB	SMT	C24F	1961	Scottish Omnibuses	1948
1958	B13-6	LST 750-3	AEC Reliance	Park Royal	DP41F	1974		
1958	E32/3	DWS 843/4	Guy Arab II	NCME	L27/26R	1966/7	Scottish Omnibuses	1944
1958	E34/39	EFS 354/6	Guy Arab II	Weymann	L27/26R	1963/5	Scottish Omnibuses	1945
1958	E40	DSG 178	Guy Arab I	Brush	L27/26R	1963	Scottish Omnibuses	1943
1958	E41/2	EFS 353/7	Guy Arab II	Weymann	L27/26R	1967/5	Scottish Omnibuses	1945
1959	B17-22	MST 800-5	AEC Reliance	Alexander	C41F	1972-6		
1959	E43	DSG 176	Guy Arab I	NCME	L27/26R	1963	Scottish Omnibuses	1943
1959	E44	DSG 179	Guy Arab I	Brush	L27/26R	1963	Scottish Omnibuses	1943
1959	C28-33	JSF 828-33	Bedford SB	Burlingham	FC30F	1963/4	Scottish Omnibuses	1952
1960	B23-7	OST 501-5	AEC Reliance	Alexander	C41F	1976/7		
1960	E67/8	ASD 404/5	Guy Arab II	NECW	L27/26RD	1965	Western SMT	1943
1960	C24	JSF 826	Bedford SB	Burlingham	FC30F	1964	Scottish Omnibuses	1952
1961	B30-5	RST 450-5	AEC Reliance	Alexander	C38F	1976/7		
1961	B28/9	ESC 430/1	AEC Regal	Duple	C35F	1965	Scottish Omnibuses	1946
1961	C6-16/21	FFS 856-67	Bedford OB	Burlingham	FC24F	1962-5	Scottish Omnibuses	1947
1961	C34-9	JSF 820-5	Bedford SB	Burlingham	FC30F	1964/5	Scottish Omnibuses	1952
1962	B37-42	SST 993-8	AEC Reliance	Alexander	C38F	1977		
1962	B35	GSC 457	AEC Regal III	Burlingham	FC35F	1963	Scottish Omnibuses	1949
1962	B43/4	ESC 451/2	AEC Regal III	Duple	C35F	1965	Scottish Omnibuses	1946
1962	B45-8	ESC 441/6-8	AEC Regal III	Duple	C35F	1964/5	Scottish Omnibuses	1946
1962	C40-5	JSF 814-9	Bedford SB	Burlingham	FC30F	1963/4	Scottish Omnibuses	1952
1963	D1	BSD 403	AEC Regent III	NCME	L27/26R	1964	Western SMT	1947
1963	E7/8/6	HGC 146-8	Guy Arab II	Alexander	L27/26RD	1966/7	Western SMT	1945
1963	K1/2	ESD 221/2	Guy Arab UF	Alexander	C30CT	1968/9	Western SMT	1953
1963	K3/7-9	EAG 893/7-9	Guy Arab UF	Alexander	C30CT	1968	Western SMT	1952
1963	K4-6	EAG 894-6	Guy Arab UF	Alexander	C35C	1968	Western SMT	1952
1963	K10-12	EAG 473/901-2	Guy Arab UF	Alexander	C35C	1968	Western SMT	1952
1963	K13	EAG 474	Guy Arab UF	Alexander	C35C	1968	Western SMT	1952
1963	L1-12	NSG 780-91	Bristol Lodekka	ECW	H33/27R	1971/2	Scottish Omnibuses	1956
1963	E9	GYL 448	Guy Arab II	NCME	H30/26R	1964	W Alexander Midland	1946
1964	CD1-8	WST 500-7	Bedford VAS1	Duple Midland	DP28F			1971-9
1964	A7	LUO 883	Albion FT3AB	Duple	C31F	1965	J Bain & Son	1950
1964	A8	CMS 354	Albion FT3AB	Strachan	C31F	1964	Ross, Balblair	1949
1964	C22	AJS 451	Bedford SB	Duple	C33F	1965	Ross, Balblair	1953
1964	A9	BJS 769	Albion FT39AL	Strachan	B33F	1968	MacKenzie, Garve	1955
1964	M2	FJS 254	Morris J2VM	Kenex	B11R	1968	MacKenzie, Garve	1959
1964	CD9	JJS 17	Bedford	Duple	C41F	1976	MacKenzie, Garve	1961
1964		SJ 1120	Bedford OB	SMT	C29F	1964	MacKintosh, Croy	1947
1964	J1	WG 9195	Leyland TD7	Leyland	L27/26R	1964	W Alexander Midland	1940
1964	D2-3	CAV 824/98	Daimler CWA6	Duple	L27/26R	1964	W Alexander Midland	1945
1964	D4	AMS 110	Daimler CWA6	Brush	L27/26R	1964	W Alexander Midland	1944
1964	K15-8/4	GVD 36-40	Guy Arab UF	Alexander	C41C	1968/9	Central SMT	1952

118

Year Rec'd	Fleet No.	Reg.No	Chassis	Body	Seating	Withdrawn	Former operator	Year New
1964	B50-2	HWS 927-8/36	AEC Regal IV	Alexander	B44F	1965	Western SMT	1951
1964	B53-4/6	HWS 933-4/7	AEC Regal IV	Alexander	B44F	1965-7	Western SMT	1951
1964	B55	HWS 939	AEC Regal IV	Alexander	B44F	1965-7	Western SMT	1951
1964	D4-6	BSD 292/461/9	Daimler CVG6	Alexander	L31/26R	1965	Western SMT	1951
1964	K21/19/20	ESD 219-21	Guy Arab UF	Alexander	C35C	1969	Western SMT	1953
1964	B57/8	GSF 690/2	AEC Regal III	Burlingham	C35F	1967	Scottish Omnibuses	1949
1964	T1	GSS 804	Ford 570E	Duple Northern	C41F	1976	Scottish Omnibuses	1963
1964	T2	FSS 929	Ford 570E	Duple Northern	C41F	1975	Scottish Omnibuses	1962
1964	T3	430 YTD	Ford 570E	Duple Northern	C41F	1976	Scottish Omnibuses	1962
1964	T4	GSS 452	Ford 570E	Duple Northern	C41F	1976	Scottish Omnibuses	1963
1965	CD11/12	BST 200/1C	Bedford VAS1	Duple Midland	C28F	1977/8		
1965	C7	VME 732	Bedford OB	Duple	C29F	1965	Achnasheen Hotel	1950
1965	C8	WMP 189	Bedford SB	Duple	C33F	1965	Achnasheen Hotel	1952
1965	CD10	FGS 872	Bedford A4LB9	Duple	C14FM	1970	Achnasheen Hotel	1954
1965	M3	HJS 245	Austin J2VA	Kenex	12	1968	Achnasheen Hotel	1960
1965	MR1	UST 298	Land Rover	Rover	11	1965	Achnasheen Hotel	1963
1965		EAG 190	Bedford SB	Duple	C33F	1965	Newton, Dingwall	1951
1965		879 EVK	Bedford SB3	Plaxton	C41F	1965	Newton, Dingwall	1958
1965	T5	3023 HX	Ford 570E	Plaxton	C41F	1968	Newton, Dingwall	1960
1965	T6	MJS 523	Ford 570E	Duple	C41F	1975	Newton, Dingwall	1963
1965	T7	BJS 440B	Ford 570E	Plaxton	C41F	1975	Newton, Dingwall	1964
1965	A12	MJS 808	Albion VT21L	Duple Northern	C41F	1968	Newton, Dingwall	1963
1965	MB1	AJS 893B	Commer 1500LBD	Harrington	12	1972	Newton, Dingwall	1964
1965	DA2/4	BMS 402/4	Daimler CVD6	Burlingham	C33F	1966/7	W Alexander Midland	1948
1965	DA5/6	DMS 560/1	Daimler CVD6	ECW	FC37F	1967	W Alexander Midland	1951
1965	DA8/9	BMS 408/16	Daimler CVD6	Burlingham	C33F	1966/7	W Alexander Midland	1948
1965	A10/11	OMS 239/47	Albion NS3L	Alexander	C29F	1968	W Alexander Midland	1960
1965	K33	AMS 549	Guy Arab III	Duple	C35F	1965	W Alexander Midland	1947
1965	B59/60	GSF 695/6	AEC Regal III	Burlingham	C35F	1967	Scottish Omnibuses	1949
1965	A12	FTS 181	Albion MR9	Plaxton	C29F	1965	W Alexander Fife	1956
1965	K22	FAG 92	Guy Arab UF	Alexander	C38C	1970	Western SMT	1953
1965	K23-32/4-6	EAG 460-72	Guy Arab UF	Alexander	C41C	1967	Western SMT	1952
1965	K38-40	EAG 475-7	Guy Arab UF	Alexander	C41C	1967-9	Western SMT	1952
1965	K41-3	EAG 478-9/92	Guy Arab UF	Alexander	C36C	1969/70	Western SMT	1952
1965	AL5/10	EGM 5/10	Albion Lowlander LR1	NCME	H39/32F	1977	Central SMT	1962
1965	AL11-9	FGM 11-9	Albion Lowlander LR1	Alexander	H41/31F	1977-9	Central SMT	1963
1965	AL21/2	FGM 21/2	Albion Lowlander LR1	NCME	H39/32F	1978	Central SMT	1963
1966	CD13	CST 961D	Bedford VAM5	Alexander	C24FM	1981		
1966	T10	DST 440D	Ford R226	Plaxton	C52F	1980		
1966	T20	DST 439D	Ford R192	Duple Midland	B45F	1979		
1966		DRS 666	Albion FT39N	Alexander	C32F	1966	Smith, Grantown	1950
1966		SO 9111	Bedford OB	Duple	C29F	1966	Smith, Grantown	1950
1966	C1	MTF 313	Bedford SB	Duple	C33F	1967	Smith, Grantown	1951
1966		ERS 400	Albion FT39N	Duple	C31F	1966	Smith, Grantown	1952
1966		JWS 125	Guy Arab rebuild	SOL	B39F	1966	Smith, Grantown	1952
1966		JSF 814	Bedford SB	Burlingham	FC30F	1966	Smith, Grantown	1952
1966	D1	NWU 660	Commer Avenger II	Plaxton	C39F	1967	Smith, Grantown	1954
1966	D2	HTY 823	Commer Avenger III	Plaxton	C39F	1968	Smith, Grantown	1955
1966	D3	PUY 485	Commer Avenger III	Duple	C41F	1967	Smith, Grantown	1956
1966	D4	SPT 106	Commer Avenger III	Plaxton	C41F	1967	Smith, Grantown	1955
1966	D5	PDA 248	Commer Avenger III	Plaxton	C41F	1967	Smith, Grantown	1955
1966	CD14	RVM 34	Befford SBO	Burlingham	FC36F	1968	Smith, Grantown	1955
1966	CD15	MSO 579	Bedford SB5	Duple	C41F	1976	Smith, Grantown	1964
1966	A1/4	KST 50/3	Albion MR9	Alexander	C29F	1967	Smith, Grantown	1956
1966	MB4	MST 902	Bedford CAV	Martin Walter	11	1968	Smith, Grantown	1959
1966	T8	5793 VU	Ford 570E	Duple	C41F	1975	Happiways	1964
1966	T9	TSN 882	Ford 570E	Duple	C41F	1975	AC Barrie	1964
1966	AL1	UCS 601	Albion Lowlander LR1	NCME	H39/32F	1977	Western SMT	1962
1966	AL2	TCS 151	Albion Lowlander LR1	Alexander	H41/31F	1977	Western SMT	1962
1966	AL3/4	UCS 610/1	Albion Lowlander LR1	NCME	H39/32F	1977	Western SMT	1963
1966	AL6/7	UCS 605/2	Albion Lowlander LR1	NCME	H39/32F	1977	Western SMT	1962
1966	AL8/9	UCS 604/3	Albion Lowlander LR1	NCME	H39/32F	1977	Western SMT	1962

Year Rec'd	Fleet No.	Reg.No	Chassis	Body	Seating	Withdrawn	Former operator	Year New
1966	AL17	UCS 606	Albion Lowlander LR1	NCME	H39/30F	1977	Western SMT	1962
1966	AL20/3-4	UCS 607-9	Albion Lowlander LR1	NCME	H39/32F	1976-7	Western SMT	1962
1966	AV1-2	DXA 402/5C	Albion VK43L	Alexander	C40F	1970	W Alexander Fife	1965
1967	CD16-8	EST 820-2E	Bedford VAM5	Alexander	C38F	1981		
1967	CD19-21	EST 823-5E	Bedford VAM5	Alexander	C41F	1981		
1967	A13	LVD 635	Albion FT39AL	Duple	C35F	1968	S MacGregor,Dornoch	1955
1967	CD22	WAW 355	Bedford SB1	Burlingham	C41F	1975	S MacGregor,Dornoch	1961
1967	MB5	NS 3922	Austin J2VA	Kenex	11	1968	S MacGregor,Dornoch	1959
1967		NS 2283	Bedford OB	Duple	C29F	1967	Peter Burr, Tongue	1949
1967	CD26	MVD 268	Bedford SBO	Duple Midland	B28FM	1970	Peter Burr, Tongue	1956
1967		SUD 826	Bedford SBG	Duple	C36F	1967	Robertson, Strathglass	1955
1967	C1	UNK 229	Bedford SBG	Thurgood	C36F	1968	Robertson, Strathglass	1955
1967	K44/5	KWO 34/41	Guy Arab UF	Duple	C37F	1972	Red & White	1952
1967	K46-9	KWO 36-8/42	Guy Arab UF	Duple	C37F	1970-2	Red & White	1952
1967	AV3-7	FGM 101-5D	Albion VK43L	Alexander	C40F	1980-1	Central SMT	1966
1967	J1/2	ECK 604/599	Leyland PSU1/13	Leyland	B44F	1971	Ribble	1952
1967	J3/4	ECK 588/92	Leyland PSU1/13	Leyland	B44F	1971	Ribble	1952
1967	J5/6	ECK 564/84	Leyland PSU1/13	Leyland	B44F	1971	Ribble	1952
1967	JD1-2	CAG 135-6	Leyland PD1	NCME	L27/26R	1967	Western SMT	1948
1967	JD3-5	GCS 222/4/6	Leyland PD2/20	NCME	L27/26R	1970/1	Western SMT	1955
1967	JD6	GCS 232	Leyland PD2/20	ECW	L27/26R	1970	Western SMT	1955
1967	JD7	GCS 233	Leyland PD2/20	NCME	L27/26R	1971	Western SMT	1955
1967	E1	FSD 458	Guy Arab rebuild	NCME	L27/26R	1968	Western SMT	1954
1967	E2/3	GCS 215/6	Guy Arab IV	NCME	L27/28R	1970/1	Western SMT	1955
1967	AL25/6	UCS 626/9	Albion Lowlander LR1	Alexander	H40/31F	1977/8	Western SMT	1963
1967	AL27/8	UCS 634/5	Albion Lowlander LR1	Alexander	H41/31F	1980	Western SMT	1963
1967	AL29/30	UCS 628/7	Albion Lowlander LR1	Alexander	H41/30F	1977/8	Western SMT	1963
1967	J7/9	BMS 218/699	Leyland PS1	Alexander	C35F	1967	W Alexander Midland	1948
1967	J8	BWG 315	Leyland PS1	Alexander	C35F	1967	W Alexander Midland	1948
1967	J10-2	AWG 555/703-4	Leyland PS1	Alexander	C35F	1967	W Alexander Fife	1947
1967	T11-4	SSA 467/9-71	Ford 570E	Duple	C39F	1973	W Alexander Northern	1960
1967	CD23-5	SSA 472-4	Bedford SB1	Duple	C39F	1973	W Alexander Northern	1960
1968	CD27-32	CST 500-5	Bedford VAS5	Willowbrook	C27F	1977-81		
1968	MB6	GST 868	Ford Transit	?	12	1974		
1968	CD33-8	GST 950-5	Bedford VAM70	Willowbrook	C41F	1976/81		
1968	T17/8	HST 48-9F	Ford R192	Willowbrook	B45F	1981		
1968	T19/21	PUS 496-7F	Ford R192	Willowbrook	B45F	1981		
1968		SX 7039	Bedford OB	Duple	C29F	1968	Kennedy, Kiltarlity	1950
1968	D1	PLF 359	Karrier	Strachan	B14F	1970	W Alexander Fife	1956
1968	T15	873 WTW	Ford 570E	Duple	C41F	1975	W Alexander Fife	1961
1968	T16	ESP 292D	Ford R192	Duple Northern	C45F	1976	W Alexander Fife	1966
1968	GL1-10	FSD 464-73	Guy Arab LUF	Alexander	C41F	1969-71	Western SMT	1954
1968	GL11-25	GCS 195-209	Guy Arab LUF	Alexander	B44F	1970-2	Western SMT	1955
1969	T22/24	KST 360/2G	Ford R192	Willowbrook	DP41F	1981/2		
1969	T23/5/5-33	KST 361/3-71G	Ford R192	Willowbrook	B45F	1981/2		
1969	BA1-10	EWS 121-30D	AEC Reliance	Alexander	C49F	1980-2	Scottish Omnibuses	1966
1969	BA11-6	EWS 135-40D	AEC Reliance	Alexander	C49F	1980-2	Scottish Omnibuses	1966
1969	L13-8	GM 7020-5	Bristol Lodekka	ECW	H29/27RD	1971/2	Central SMT	1955
1969	JD8	MVA 100	Leyland PD2/12	NCME	L27/28R	1970	Central SMT	1955
1969	JD9	OVD 950	Leyland PD2/20	NCME	L31/28R	1971	Central SMT	1957
1970	T34/5	MST 934-5J	Ford R192	Willowbrook	B45F	1982		
1970	T36/7	MST 36-7H	Ford R192	Willowbrook	B45F	1982		
1970	T38/9	MST 938/46J	Ford R192	Willowbrook	B45F	1982		
1970	T40-2	MST 40-2H	Ford R192	Willowbrook	B45F	1982		
1970	T43-5	MST 943-5J	Ford R192	Willowbrook	B45F	1982		
1970	CD75	NST 175J	Bedford SB5	Willowbrook	B39F	1981		
1970	B43	UGB 428	AEC Reliance	Duple Midland	C41F	1976	David MacBrayne	1958
1970	B44/5	XGD 775/6	AEC Reliance	Park Royal	B45F	1976	David MacBrayne	1959
1970	B46/7	XGB 434/5	AEC Reliance	Duple Midland	C41F	1976	David MacBrayne	1959
1970	B48-50	WGG 634-6	AEC Reliance	Duple Midland	C41F	1976	David MacBrayne	1959
1970	B51/2	293/4 AGE	AEC Reliance	Duple Midland	C41F	1977	David MacBrayne	1960
1970	B53	195 CUS	AEC Reliance	Duple Midland	C43F	1977	David MacBrayne	1961

Year Rec'd	Fleet No.	Reg.No	Chassis	Body	Seating	Withdrawn	Former operator	Year New
1970	B54/5	197/9 CUS	AEC Reliance	Duple Midland	C41F	1976/7	David MacBrayne	1961
1970	B56	200 CUS	AEC Reliance	Duple Midland	B44F	1976	David MacBrayne	1961
1970	B57/8	387/9 FGB	AEC Reliance	Duple Midland	B44F	1976	David MacBrayne	1962
1970	B59-60	390/1 FGB	AEC Reliance	Duple Midland	C41F	1976/7	David MacBrayne	1962
1970	B61/2	EYS 61/3C	AEC Reliance	Duple Northern	C43F	1979	David MacBrayne	1965
1970	B63	196 CUS	AEC Reliance	Duple Midland	C43F	1979	David MacBrayne	1965
1970	B64	198 CUS	AEC Reliance	Duple Midland	C41F	1979	David MacBrayne	1965
1970	B65/6	388/92 FGB	AEC Reliance	Duple Midland	C41F	1976/7	David MacBrayne	1962
1970	B67	422 JGB	AEC Reliance	Duple	C45F	1979	David MacBrayne	1963
1970	B68-70	AGE 545-7B	AEC Reliance	Duple	C43F	1979	David MacBrayne	1964
1970	B71	EYS 62C	AEC Reliance	Duple Northern	C43F	1979	David MacBrayne	1965
1970	BA17	CGA 585B	AEC Reliance	Duple Northern	B53F	1978	David MacBrayne	1964
1970	BA18	CGA 586B	AEC Reliance	Willowbrook	B53F	1978	David MacBrayne	1964
1970	BA19	EGB 885C	AEC Reliance	Willowbrook	B53F	1980	David MacBrayne	1965
1970	BA20	LUS 524E	AEC Reliance	Willowbrook	C49F	1981	David MacBrayne	1967
1970	BA21	UGB 697H	AEC Reliance	Willowbrook	B45F	1981	David MacBrayne	1969
1970	BA22	UGB 698H	AEC Reliance	Willowbrook	B53F	1981	David MacBrayne	1969
1970	BA23/4	PGB 708/9F	AEC Reliance	Duple Northern	C43F	1981	David MacBrayne	1968
1970	BA25	PGE 429F	AEC Reliance	Willowbrook	C49F	1981	David MacBrayne	1968
1970		3288 WB		Plaxton	C41F	1970	David MacBrayne	1958
1970		8332 U	AEC Reliance	Plaxton	C41C	1970	David MacBrayne	1958
1970		119 GMA	Ford 570E	Duple	C41F	1970	David MacBrayne	1959
1970	C1-5	WGG 621-5	Bedford C5ZI	Duple Midland	B28F	1970	David MacBrayne	1959
1970	C6-8	WGG 631-3	Bedford C5ZI	Duple	C29F	1970	David MacBrayne	1959
1970	C9-12	YYS 175-9	Bedford C5ZI	Duple	C29F	1970	David MacBrayne	1960
1970	C13-8	603/4/6-9 CYS	Bedford C5CI	Duple	C29F	1970	David MacBrayne	1961
1971	C19	WGG 622	Bedford C5ZI	Duple Midland	B28F	1971	David MacBrayne	1959
1971	C20	WGG 545	Bedford C5ZI	Duple	C29F	1971	David MacBrayne	1959
1971	C26/7	YYS 178/80	Bedford C5ZI	Duple	C29F	1972	David MacBrayne	1960
1971	C28/9	605/10 CYS	Bedford C5CI	Duple	C29F	1972	David MacBrayne	1961
1971		WGG 625	Bedford C5ZI	Duple Midland	B28F	1971	David MacBrayne	1959
1971		WGG 629/30	Bedford C5ZI	Duple	C29F	1971	David MacBrayne	1959
1971	CD39-40	PGD 215-6F	Bedford SB5	Plaxton	C41F	1979	David MacBrayne	1968
1971	CD41	UGB 138H	Bedford SB5	Willowbrook	B40F	1981	David MacBrayne	1969
1971	CD42-4	372/5/6 FGB	Bedford VASI	Duple	C29F	1976/7	David MacBrayne	1962
1971	CD45-7	377/81/2 FGB	Bedford VASI	Duple Midland	B30F	1973	David MacBrayne	1962
1971	CD48	384 FGB	Bedford VASI	Duple Midland	B13FM	1971	David MacBrayne	1962
1971	CD49	386 FGB	Bedford VASI	Duple Midland	B21F	1973	David MacBrayne	1962
1971	CD50	845 HUS	Bedford VASI	Duple Northern	B29F	1974	David MacBrayne	1963
1971	CD51	846 HUS	Bedford VASI	Duple Northern	B30F	1972	David MacBrayne	1963
1971	CD52	848 HUS	Bedford VASI	Duple Northern	B24FM	1973	David MacBrayne	1963
1971	CD53	849 HUS	Bedford VASI	Duple Northern	B30F	1973	David MacBrayne	1963
1971	CD54-7	AYS 733-4/7/8B	Bedford VASI	Duple Midland	B28F	1973	David MacBrayne	1964
1971	CD58-64	EGA 826-31/3C	Bedford VASI	Duple Midland	B29F	1974-6	David MacBrayne	1965
1971	CD66-9	HGA 976-8/80-1D	Bedford VASI	Willowbrook	B28F	1973-7	David MacBrayne	1966
1971	CD70/1	HGA 982/4D	Bedford VASI	Willowbrook	B24FM	1976-7	David MacBrayne	1966
1971	CD76	847 HUS	Bedford VASI	Duple Northern	B28F	1973	David MacBrayne	1963
1971	CD79	EGA 832C	Bedford VASI	Duple Midland	B29F	1973	David MacBrayne	1965
1971	CD80-3	MGB 284-7E	Bedford SB5	Plaxton	C41F	1976-80	David MacBrayne	1967
1971	CD84-7	PGD 217-20F	Bedford SB5	Plaxton	C41F	1976/80	David MacBrayne	1968
1971	CD88	TGB 676G	Bedford SB5	Plaxton	C41F	1980	David MacBrayne	1969
1971	CD89	UGB 137H	Bedford SB5	Willowbrook	B40F	1981	David MacBrayne	1969
1971	CD90	WGE 71H	Bedford SB5	Plaxton	C41F	1980	David MacBrayne	1970
1971	CD91	HGA 979D	Bedford VASI	Willowbrook	B28F	1975	David MacBrayne	1966
1972	CD92	385 FGB	Bedford VASI	Duple Midland	B21F	1972	David MacBrayne	1962
1972	CD93	HGA 983D	Bedford VASI	Willowbrook	B24FM	1978	David MacBrayne	1966
1970		HGA 177	Bedford SB	Duple	C33F	1970	Morrison, Harris	1951
1970		EMS 829	Bedford SB	Burlingham	C31F	1970	Morrison, Harris	1953
1970	CD77	TVA 815	Bedford SB3	Plaxton	B39F	1971	Morrison, Harris	1959
1970	CD78	FYJ 847	Bedford SBG	Plaxton	C38F	1971	Morrison, Harris	1957
1970	CD72-4	YWS 866-8	Bedford VASI	Duple	C24F	1974/7	Scottish Omnibuses	1962
1970		DSN 491	Leyland PSUC1/2	Alexander	C41F	1970	W Alexander Midland	1954
1970		JMS 214/5	Leyland PSUC1/2	Alexander	B45F	1970	W Alexander Midland	1956

Year Rec'd	Fleet No.	Reg.No	Chassis	Body	Seating	Withdrawn	Former operator	Year New
1970		MWG 412	Leyland PSUC1/2	Alexander	C41F	1970	W Alexander Midland	1959
1970	B78	RMS 737	AEC Reliance	Alexander	C41F	1977	W Alexander Midland	1961
1970		TWG581/3-4/94	Leyland PSUC1/2	Alexander	C41F	1970	W Alexander Midland	1962
1970	JL1	AMS 293B	Leyland PSU3/3R	Alexander	B53F	1977	W Alexander Midland	1964
1970	AV8	JMS 439E	Albion VK43AL	Alexander	C40F	1981	W Alexander Midland	1967
1970	AV9	NMS 128F	Albion VK43AL	Alexander	C40F	1980	W Alexander Midland	1968
1970	SL1	SWG 678H	Bristol LH6P	Alexander	C41F	1971	W Alexander Midland	1970
1970	B72-4	GWG 470/4/7	AEC Monocoach	Alexander	B45F	1972-4	W Alexander Midland	1955
1970	B75	OMS 290	AEC Reliance	Alexander	C37F	1977	W Alexander Midland	1960
1970	B76/7	RMS 727/33	AEC Reliance	Alexander	C41F	1977	W Alexander Midland	1961
1970	B79-81	RMS 738/9/42	AECReliance	Alexander	C41F	1975-7	W Alexander Midland	1961
1971	SL2/3	DSD 701/2D	Bristol RELH	Alexander	C38FT	1978	Western SMT	1966
1971	T46-54	PST 646-54K	Ford R192	Willowbrook	B45F	1982		
1971	SL4-10	JSD 907-9/16-9	Bristol LS	Alexander	C41F	1974	Western SMT	1957
1971	AL31-7	AAG 406-12B	Albion Lowlander LR7	Alexander	H40/29F	1977-80	Western SMT	1964
1971	AL38-42	BCS 253-7C	Albion Lowlander LR7	NCME	H39/30F	1981	Western SMT	1965
1972	T55-8	SST 255-8K	Ford R192	Willowbrook	B45F	1982/3		
1972	T59/62-4	SST 259/62-4K	Ford R192	Willowbrook	DP41F	1982/3		
1972	T65/6	SST 265-6K	Ford R192	Willowbrook	B45F	1982		
1973	T67	UST 867L	Ford R1114	Duple	C49F	1982		
1973	T68-73	UST 868-73L	Ford R1014	Willowbrook	DP41F	1982/3		
1973	T74-82	UST 874-82L	Ford R1014	Willowbrook	B43F	1982/3		
1973	T83	UST 883L	Ford R1014	Willowbrook	B46F	1982		
1973	JL2-5	VST 752-5L	Leyland PSU3/3R	Alexander	C49F	1977		
1973	HH548	OWS 548	Leyland PD2/20	Park Royal	L27/29R	1973	Scottish Omnibuses	1957
1973	AA582	OWS 582	Bristol Lodekka	ECW	H33/27R	1973	Scottish Omnibuses	1957
1973	BB1	78 BVD	AEC Bridgemaster	Park Royal	H43/29F	1976	Scottish Omnibuses	1961
1973	BB2	9962 SF	AEC Bridgemaster	Park Royal	H41/29F	1976	Scottish Omnibuses	1963
1973	BB3	9963 SF	AEC Renown	Park Royal	H42/32F	1976	Scottish Omnibuses	1963
1973	BA26-31	EWS 115-20D	AEC Reliance	Alexander	DP49F	1979-81	Scottish Omnibuses	1966
1973	NRB161-4	DWG 917-20	Leyland PD2/12	Alexander	L27/26R	1973/4	W Alexander Northern	1953
1973	NRB172	GCS 234	Leyland PD2/20	NCME	L27/28R	1973	W Alexander Northern	1955
1973	AL43	TWG 569	Albion Lowlander LR1	Alexander	H40/31F	1978	W Alexander Midland	1963
1973	CD45-9	HGM 32-6E	Bedford VAM5	Duple	C45F	1981	Central SMT	1967
1974	T84-9	BST 884-9M	Ford R1114	Alexander	C49F	1984		
1974	T90-9	CST 700-9N	Ford R1114	Alexander	B53F	1984		
1974	T11	NPM 323F	Ford R226	Strachan	DP53F	1980	Irvine, Law	1968
1974	AL44/46	EGM 2/4	Albion Lowlander LR1	Alexander	H39/32F	1977	W Alexander Fife	1962
1974	AL45	166 EMJ	Albion Lowlander LR7	East Lancs	H35/30F	1977	Ementon, Cranfield	1963
1974	HB1-4	SWS 261-4	Leyland PD3/3	Alexander	H41/31F	1976	Edinburgh Corporation	1959
1974	HB5	PWS 998	Leyland PD3/2	Alexander	H42/30F	1976	Edinburgh Corporation	1957
1974	HB6	PWS 999	Leyland PD3/2	Alexander	H41/31F	1976	Edinburgh Corporation	1959
1975	T100-5	HST 200-5N	Ford R1114	Alexander	C49F	1985-7		
1975	T106-15	JST 106-15P	Ford R1114	Alexander	B53F	1987		
1975		FMS 753-4	AEC Reliance	Alexander	B45F	1975	W Alexander Northern	1955
1975		HMS 235/41/5	AEC Reliance	Alexander	B45F	1975	W Alexander Northern	1956
1975		JMS 50	AEC Reliance	Alexander	B45F	1975	W Alexander Northern	1956
1975	AL47	TWG 555	Albion Lowlander LR1	Alexander	H40/31F	1977	W Alexander Midland	1963
1975	AL48	VWG 366	Albion Lowlander LR1	Alexander	H40/31F	1978	W Alexander Midland	1963
1975	AL49	BCS 252C	Albion Lowlander LR1	NCME	H39/30F	1981	Western SMT	1965
1976	T116-9	KST 116-9P	Ford R1014	Duple		C45F	1987	
1976	T120-5	LAS 120-5P	Ford R1114	Duple		C49F	1986-7	
1976	AL50/53	VWG 372/4	Albion Lowlander LR1	Alexander	H40/31F	220	W Alexander Midland	1963
1976	AL51	TWG 560	Albion Lowlander LR1	Alexander	H40/31F	1977	W Alexander Midland	1963
1976	AL52	VWG 376	Albion Lowlander LR1	Alexander	H40/31F	1979	W Alexander Midland	1963
1977	T126-39	MST 126-39R	Ford R1114	Duple	C49F	1985-7		
1977	T140-41	NAS 140/1R	Ford R1114	Duple	B53F	1988		
1977	T142/4	OST 224/5S	Ford R1114	Duple	B53F	1986/8		
1977	T143/5-7	NAS 143/5-7R	Ford R1114	Duple	B53F	1985-7		
1977	T148-61	OST 248-61S	Ford R1114	Duple	B53F	1985-9		
1977	CD94/5	SMS 833/4H	Bedford VAS5	Duple	C29F	1981	W Alexander Midland	1970
1977	D1/2	HXA 623/30H	Daimler CRG6LX	Alexander	H44/31F	1985	W Alexander Fife	1970

Year Rec'd	Fleet No.	Reg.No	Chassis	Body	Seating	Withdrawn	Former operator	Year New
1977	D3/4	HXA 621/2H	Daimler CRG6LX	Alexander	H44/31F	1984/5	W Alexander Fife	1970
1977	D5/6	HXA 627/32H	Daimler CRG6LX	Alexander	H44/31F	1984/5	W Alexander Fife	1970
1977	T12-6	VRG 140-4L	Ford R1114	Alexander	C49F	1983	W Alexander Northern	1972
1978	D7-10	UAG 130-3J	Daimler CRG6LX	NCME	H44/31F	1985-7	Western SMT	1971
1978	D11/2	UCS 289/90K	Daimler CRG6LX	NCME	H44/31F	1987/8	Western SMT	1971
1978	D13-8	SAS 855-60T	Leyland FE30AGR	ECW	H43/32F			
1978		JFG 404F	Bedford VAM70	Duple	C45F	1978	Greigs Garage	1968
1978		XUJ 488K	Ford R226	Caetano	C53F	1978	Greigs Garage	1972
1979	D19-27	UAS 63-71T	Leyland FE30AGR	ECW	H43/32F			
1979	T162-3	UST 2/3T	Ford R1114	Duple	C49F	1985		
1979	T164-5	VST 223/4V	Ford R1114	Duple	C49F	1989		
1979		ERG 111D	Daimler CRG6LX	Alexander	H45/34F	1979	Grampian Regional	1966
1979	T166/7	AXA 301/2N	Ford R1014	Duple	C45F	1986	W Alexander Fife	1974
1979	T168-70	HSF 549-51N	Ford R1014	Duple	C45F	1986	W Alexander Fife	1975
1980	N1-8	WAS 764-71V	Leyland National 2	Leyland	B52F	1986		
1980	T171-4	WST 815-8	Ford R1114	Duple	C49F	1990		
1980	G1-8	KSF 1-8N	Ailsa B55-10	Alexander	H44/35F	1990	W Alexander Fife	1975
1980	G9/10	LSX 9/10P	Ailsa B55-10	Alexander	H44/35F	1990	W Alexander Fife	1975
1981	N9-18	AST 151-60W	Leyland National 2	Leyland	B52F	1985/6		
1981	L17-24	CAS 511-8W	Leyland PSU3G/4R	Alexander	C49F			
1981	L25/6	CAS 519/20W	Leyland PSU3G/4R	Alexander	C49F	1985		
1981	G11	YMS 714R	Ailsa B55-10	Alexander	H44/35F	1990	W Alexander Midland	1977
1981	L1-3	RSD 728-9/31J	Leyland PSU3/3R	Alexander	DP49F	1983	Western SMT	1971
1981	L4	RSD 732J	Leyland PSU3/3R	Alexander	B53F	1983	Western SMT	1971
1981	L5-9	RSD 733/4/7-9J	Leyland PSU3/3R	Alexander	DP49F	1983	Western SMT	1971
1981	L10/11	RSD 748/9J	Leyland PSU3/3R	Alexander	DP49F	1983	Western SMT	1971
1981		CAG 453/70C	Leyland PSU3/3R	Alexander	DP49F	1981	Central SMT	1965
1981	CD96/7	KGG 718/9N	Bedford VAS5	Duple	C27F	1983	Central SMT	1975
1981	L12-4	GSO 77-9V	Leyland PSU3/3R	Alexander	B53F			
1981	L15-6	GSO 80-1V	Leyland PSU3/3R	Alexander	B53F	1983		
1981		HWG 501E	Daimler CRG6LX	Alexander	H44/31F	1981	W Alexander Midland	1967
1982	L27	FAS 372X	Leyland PSU3/4R	Alexander	B62F			
1982	L28-31	FAS 373-6X	Leyland PSU3F/4R	Alexander	B62F			
1982	D28-32	PXA 635-8/40J	Daimler CRG6LX	ECW	H43/34F	1984/7	W Alexander Fife	1971
1982	D33-7	PXA 642-4/6/7J	Daimler CRG6LX	ECW	H43/34F	1987	W Alexander Fife	1971
1982	T175-81	HSF 556-62N	Ford R1114	Alexander	B53F	1987	W Alexander Fife	1975
1982	L44-8	CFS 105-9S	Leyland PSU3E/4R	Duple	C49F	1990	W Alexander Fife	1978
1982	L49	CFS 111	Leyland PSU3E/4R	Duple	C49F	1985	W Alexander Fife	1978
1982	T182	RWG 955N	Ford	Alexander	B53F	1984	W Alexander Midland	1974
1982	L32/3	GLS 282/3N	Leyland PSU3/3R	Alexander	B53F	1986	W Alexander Midland	1974
1982	L34-6	YSD 337/43/4L	Leyland PSU3/3R	Alexander	DP49F	1984/5	Western SMT	1973
1982	L37-42	YSD 352-6/63L	Leyland PSU3/3R	Alexander	DP49F	1984/5	Western SMT	1973
1982	L43	YSD 358L	Leyland PSU3/3R	Alexander	DP49F	1985	Western SMT	1973
1982	E1	PRN 125X	Leyland TRCT11/3R	Duple	C49FT		Duple Demonstrator	1982
1983	L50	GSO 534N	Leyland PSU5S/4R	Alexander	C42FT	1984	W Alexander Northern	1975
1983	D38/46	TGM 201/4J	Daimler CRG6LX	ECW	H43/34F	1987	Scottish Omnibuses	1971
1983	D47-9	TGM 207/9/12J	Daimler CRG6LX	ECW	H43/34F	1988-9	Scottish Omnibuses	1971
1983	D40/1	TGM 213/5J	Daimler CRG6LX	ECW	H43/34F	1986/7	Scottish Omnibuses	1971
1983	D39/42/3	TGM 217-9J	Daimler CRG6LX	ECW	H43/34F	1987/9	Scottish Omnibuses	1971
1983	D44/5	KWG 359/67F	Daimler CRG6LX	Alexander	H44/31F	1989	W Alexander Midland	1984
1983	D50/1	MLH 440/1L	Daimler CRL6	MCW	H44/29F	1989	Western SMT	1973
1983	L51/2	WFS 152/3W	Leyland PSU3F/4R	Alexander	B62F		W Alexander Fife	1980
1983	J1-6	A976-80 OST	Leyland ONLXB/1R	Alexander	H45/32F			
1983	E2-5	A504-7 PST	Leyland TRCT11/3R	Duple	C46FT			
1984	L53/6	SCS 337-9/41M	Leyland PSU3/3R	Alexander	DP49F	1985/6	Western SMT	1974
1984	L57/60	SCS 343/8M	Leyland PSU3/3R	Alexander	B53F	1985	Western SMT	1974
1984	L58/9	SCS 346/7N	Leyland PSU3/3R	Alexander	DP49F	1985	Western SMT	1974
1984	L61-4	SCS 351/2/4/6N	Leyland PSU3/3R	Alexander	B53F	1985/6	Western SMT	1974
1984	L65/6	SCS 362/4N	Leyland PSU3/3R	Alexander	B53F	1986	Western SMT	1974
1984	L67	GCS 793N	Leyland PSU3/3R	Alexander	C49F	1985	Western SMT	1975
1984	A1-5	NRG 165/7-70M	Leyland AN68/1R	Alexander	H45/29F	1988	Grampian Regional	1973
1985	J7-15	B891-9 UAS	Leyland ONLXB/1R	Alexander	H45/32F			

Year Rec'd	Fleet No.	Reg.No	Chassis	Body	Seating	Withdrawn	Former operator	Year New
1985	E6-11	B870-5 UST	Leyland TRCT11/3R	Duple	C46FT			
1985	L68/9	GLS 286/9N	Leyland PSU3/3R	Alexander	B53F	1985	W Alexander Midland	1985
1985	L70	OLS 536P	Leyland PSU3/3R	Alexander	B53F	1985	W Alexander Midland	1985
1985	V816/7	B816/7 FJS	Volvo B10M-61	Van Hool	C52FT		Newton, Dingwall	1984
1985	V834	4234 NT	Volvo B10M-61	Van Hool	C52FT		Newton, Dingwall	1984
1985	V880	2080 NT	Volvo B10M-61	Van Hool	C52FT		Newton, Dingwall	1984
1985	V883	1983 NT	Volvo B10M-61	Van Hool	C52FT		Newton, Dingwall	1984
1985	V892	3692 NT	Volvo B10M-61	Van Hool	C52FT		Newton, Dingwall	1984
1985	R924/5	B924/5 BGA	Volvo B10MT-53	Plaxton	CH55/9FT	1986	Newton, Dingwall	1985
1985	A972/82/7	JSC 872/82/7E	Leyland PDR1/1	Alexander	H43/31F	1987	Newton, Dingwall	1967
1985	K981	EAG 981D	Daimler CRG6LX	Alexander	H44/31F	1986	Newton, Dingwall	1966
1986	E882	A182 UGB	Leyland TRCLXC/2RH	Plaxton	C49F		Western SMT	1984
1986	E893	A183 UGB	Leyland TRCLXC/2RH	Plaxton	C49F	1990	Western SMT	1984
1986	L803	LMS 383W	Leyland PSU3E/4R	Alexander	B53F		Kelvin Scottish	1980
1986	L833/7	ULS 333/7T	Leyland PSU3E/4R	Alexander	B53F		Kelvin Scottish	1979
1986	L854	DLS 354V	Leyland PSU3E/4R	Alexander	B53F	1990	Kelvin Scottish	1979
1986	L857	DLS 357V	Leyland PSU3E/4R	Alexander	B53F		Kelvin Scottish	1979
1986	L872/5	LMS 372/5W	Leyland PSU3E/4R	Alexander	DP49F		Kelvin Scottish	1980
1986	L873	LMS 373W	Leyland PSU3E/4R	Alexander	B53F		Kelvin Scottish	1980
1986	L804	TMS 404X	Leyland PSU3G/4R	Alexander	B53F		Kelvin Scottish	1982
1986	L805-7	TMS 405-7X	Leyland PSU3G/4R	Alexander	DP49F		Kelvin Scottish	1982
1986	L820/2/3	TMS 420/2/3X	Leyland PSU3G/4R	Alexander	B53F		Kelvin Scottish	1982
1986	F372-7	C372-7 CAS	Leyland ONLXB/1R	Alexander	CH47/25F			
1986	J378-80	C378-80 CAS	Leyland ONLXB/1R	Alexander	H45/34F			
1986	R952	A852 TDS	Volvo B10M-61	Van Hool	CH49/9FT		Clydeside Scottish	1984
1986	R999	A199 WUS	Volvo B10M-61	Van Hool	CH49/9FT		Clydeside Scottish	1984
1987	E271-5	D271-5 FAS	Leyland TRCT11/3R	Duple	C49FT			
1987	E276-9	D276-9 FAS	Leyland TRCT11/3R	Alexander	C53F	1987		
1987	K942-6	VRS 142-4/6L	Daimler CRL6	Alexander	H45/29D	1989	Strathtay Scottish	1973
1987	K947/8	VRS 147/8	Daimler CRL6	Alexander	H45/36F	1989	W Alexander Fife	1973
1987	K954/62	PYJ 444/2L	Daimler CRG6LXB-33	Alexander	H49/37F	1989	W Alexander Fife	1972
1987	H10	PYJ 443L	Daimler CRG6LXB-33	Alexander	H49/37F	1989	W Alexander Fife	1972
1988	Q401-5	E401-5 TBS	Renault S56	Alexander	B25F			
1988	D920/3/8	SMS 120/3/8P	Daimler CRG6LXB	Alexander	H44/31F		W Alexander Fife	1976
1988	L876/13	YSF 76/83S	Leyland PSU3D/4R	Alexander	B53F		W Alexander Fife	1977
1988	L884/90	YSF 84/90S	Leyland PSU3D/4R	Alexander	B53F		W Alexander Fife	1977
1988	L891	YSF 91S	Leyland PSU3E/4R	Alexander	B53F		W Alexander Fife	1977
1988	L895	YSF 95S	Leyland PSU3D/4R	Alexander	B53F		W Alexander Fife	1977
1988	L830	GSG 120T	Leyland PSU3E/4R	Alexander	C49F		W Alexander Fife	1978
1988	L825/8	GSG 125/8T	Leyland PSU3E/4R	Alexander	C49F		W Alexander Fife	1978
1988	L836/43	GCS 36/43V	Leyland PSU3E/4R	Alexander	B53F		Clydeside Scottish	1980
1988	L852/63	GCS 52/63V	Leyland PSU3E/4R	Alexander	B53F		Clydeside Scottish	1980
1988	L867-9	XSG 67-9R	Leyland PSU3E/4R	Alexander	B53F		Midland Scottish	1977
1988	L814	YSF 104S	Leyland PSU3E/4R	Alexander	B53F		Midland Scottish	1977
1988	P777	E77 TDA	Metrorider	MCW	B25F		Ex Demonstrator	1988
1989	P1	E911 AFM	Mercedes Benz 609D	Scott	C24F		Whitelaw, Stonehouse	1987
1989	P2	E434 YSU	Mercedes Benz 609D	Scott	C24F		Whitelaw, Stonehouse	1987
1989	P3/4	D153/4 NON	Freight Rover 365		B20F			1986
1989	P6	D246 OOJ	Freight Rover 365		B18F			1986
1990	Q406/7	D316/7 MHS	Dodge S56	Alexander	B21F		Kelvin Scottish	1986
1990	Q408-12	D818-22 RYS	Dodge S56	Alexander	B25F		Kelvin Scottish	1986
1990	E276-9	D323 RNS	Leyland TRCT11/3R	Duple	C46FT		Kelvin Scottish	1987
1990	D924/5	SMS 124/5P	Daimler CRG6LXB	Alexander	H44/31F		Fife Scottish	1976
1990	D929/30	SMS 129/30P	Daimler CRG6LXB	Alexander	H44/31F		Fife Scottish	1976
1990	L877/8	YSF 77/8S	Leyland PSU3D/4R	Alexander	B53F		Fife Scottish	1977
1990	L893	YSF 103S	Leyland PSU3E/4R	Alexander	B53F		Fife Scottish	1977
1990	L894	YSF 94S	Leyland PSU3E/4R	Alexander	B53F		Fife Scottish	1977
1990	L896	YSF 96S	Leyland PSU3D/4R	Alexander	B53F		Fife Scottish	1977

Number 40, ST 5674, was an Albion PJ26 which had been converted to a breakdown truck. (ABC)

Number 31, ST 4712, a 1927 Albion PM28 after conversion to a 5 ton lorry. (ABC)

Number 95, SK 2433 is being loaded with mailbags at Thurso Station. This Fordson BB was new to J Wilson of Thurso in August 1940 and passed to Highland in October that same year and was promptly converted to a 2 ton lorry.

Number C95. Originally an SMT bus, this Bedford OWB was converted to a lorry and is collecting mailbags at Thurso. (IMc)

Number H8. This Leyland TS7 has just been converted to a breakdown truck and is inside Carse Road depot.

LSC 467, a Bedford parcels delivery van, is outside the tours office in Thurso.

At Dingwall garage is Bedford 5 ton lorry, DJS 896 (H3) which was used for deliveries to the West Coast.

AGM 692L is at Seafield depot and numbered H1 in the service fleet.

Dunnet Head lighthouse, which is the most northerly point of the British mainland, forms the attractive backdrop to this view of T94, a Ford R1114 with Alexander body. It was working the service from Thurso to John O'Groats.

In course of preparation

NORTHERN ROADWAYS

by

Garry Ward

The story of this Glasgow based operator with all the ramifications of bus, coach and contract work. Fully illustrated including timetables and memorabilia.

Expected late 2008 c£12

Venture *publications*

128 PIKES LANE GLOSSOP DERBYSHIRE SK13 8EH ☎01457 861508
E-MAIL info@venturepublications.co.uk INTERNET www.venturepublications.co.uk

ISBN 978-1-905304-18-9

ISBN 978 190530 4189

£17.95

9 781905 304189